ROCKING THE BOAT

PAUL LANDAIS-STAMP AND PAUL ROGERS

Rocking the Boat

New Zealand, the United States and the
Nuclear-Free Zone Controversy in the 1980s

BERG

Oxford / New York / Munich
Distributed exclusively in the US and Canada by
St Martin's Press, New York

First published in 1989 by
Berg Publishers Limited
Editorial Offices:
77 Morrell Avenue, Oxford OX4 INQ, UK
165 Taber Avenue, Providence R.I. 02906, USA
Westermühlstraße 26, 8000 München 5, FRG

British Library Cataloguing in Publication Data
Nuclear powered ships. Berthing. Policies of New Zealand
government, 1984–1988
623.825
ISBN 0–85496–297–4

Library of Congress Cataloging-in-Publication Data
Landais-Stamp, Paul.
    Rocking the boat: New Zealand, the United States and the Nuclear-Free
    zone Controversy in the 1980s
    Paul Landais-Stamp and Paul Rogers.
        p.   cm.
    Includes index.
    Bibliography: p.
    ISBN 0–85496–279–4
    1. New Zealand—Military policy. 2. Nuclear warships—Government
policy—New Zealand. 3. Nuclear weapons—Government policy—New
Zealand. 4. New Zealand—Military relations—United States.
5. United States—Military relations—New Zealand. I. Rogers,
Paul. II. Title.
UA874.3.L36 1989
355′.0335′931—dc19   89–152
                                                                             CIP

Printed in Great Britain by Billing and Sons Ltd, Worcester

Contents

The Authors

Paul Landais-Stamp took a degree in Peace Studies at Bradford University and is currently engaged in research there on processes of mediation in international conflict. He travelled widely in New Zealand in 1986–7 when working on this book.

Paul Rogers has taught in the Department of Peace Studies at Bradford for ten years. He chaired the UK Alternative Defence Commission from 1984–7 and wrote the Commission's evidence submitted to the Committee of Enquiry on the Future of New Zealand Strategic and Security Policies in 1986. He is also the author of *Guide to Nuclear Weapons* (Berg Publishers, Oxford and New York, 1988).

We believe that those who live by freedom and benefit from freedom ought to be willing to defend it, so we're disappointed in that aspect of the New Zealand performance.

US Secretary of State George Shultz
February 1985

We hope the Socialist bums ensconced in Wellington will get thrown out as they predictably botch both the domestic and foreign policy of a great nation.

New York Tribune
February 1985

The United States has been forthright and straightforward. It has told us its position, and we have told it ours. We can work that through, and we will work it through because the United States understands . . . that there is more to our relationship than nuclear weapons.

New Zealand Prime Minister David Lange
February 1985

The New Zealand Government does not see why "solidarity" in an alliance always means agreeing with the American view.

New Zealand Deputy Prime Minister
Geoffrey Palmer
March 1985

To compel an ally to accept nuclear weapons against the wishes of that ally is to take the moral position of totalitarianism, which allows for no self-determination.

New Zealand Prime Minister David Lange
The Oxford Union Debate, March 1985

Sometimes it is more difficult to deal with a messy democracy like New Zealand than with some Asian dictatorships.

US Ambassador to New Zealand Paul Cleveland
September 1986

To ensure that there is no misunderstanding I think it best to say clearly that as between the United States and New Zealand the security alliance is a dead letter. . . . This raises the issue of whether New Zealand should give formal notice of withdrawal from the ANZUS Council . . .

New Zealand Prime Minister David Lange
Yale University, April 1989

There is not and cannot be any security alliance between the United States and New Zealand. There can be no going back to the way it was.

New Zealand Prime Minister David Lange
Yale University, April 1989

Acknowledgements

Much of the research for this book was conducted during a five month trip to New Zealand between December 1986 and April 1987. We are indebted to many people in New Zealand for help and advice in compiling the information for this book. In particular, we would like to thank the following people for their valuable insights: Carol Dee, Betty and Gerald Fowler, June Gregg, Nicky Hager, Richard Harward, Iain McDougall, Llwewlyn Richards, Larry Ross, Sandra Shearn, Les Slater, Ron Smith, Lisa Thompson and Owen Wilkes. The responsibility for the interpretation and use of the material they provided rests, of course, with the authors.

Paul Landais-Stamp would also like to express his thanks to Dr Malcolm Dando, and his gratitude to the McKinley Travel Fund and The Quaker Peace and Service Trust for their generous travel scholarships which helped to pay for his trip to New Zealand. In this context, too, John Henkel and Dr Tom Woodhouse deserve special mention.

Thanks are also due to Julie Cox for her prompt and efficient typing of much of the manuscript, and to the University of Bradford graphics department for the map artwork.

Abbreviations

AAFLI	Asian-American Free Labor Institute
ACTU	Australian Council of Trade Unionists
AMPART	American Participants (Program)
ANZUS	Australia, New Zealand, United States (alliance/Treaty)
ASEAN	Association of South-East Asian Nations
CANWAR	Coalition Against Nuclear Warships
CARE	Citizens' Association for Racial Equality
CENTCOM	Central Command
CER	Closer Economic Relations (Agreement)
CSIS	Center for Strategic and International Studies
DGSE	Direction générale de la sécurité extérieure
FOIA	Freedom of Information Act
GLCM	Ground-Launched Cruise Missile
HART	Halt All Racist Tours
ICBM	Intercontinental Ballistic Missile
INF	Intermediate Nuclear Force (Treaty)
IV(P)	International Visitor (Program)
JRDTF	Joint Rapid Deployment Task Force
MIRV	Multiple Independently Targetable Re-entry Vehicle
NED	National Endowment for Democracy
NWFZ	Nuclear Weapon Free Zone
NZFOL	New Zealand Federation of Labour
NZNFZC	New Zealand Nuclear Free Zone Committee
OPEC	Organisation of Petroleum Exporting Countries
PDU	Pacific Democratic Union
SALT	Strategic Arms Limitation Talks
SDI	Strategic Defense Initiative
SEAL	Sea-Air-Land (forces)

Abbreviations

SEATO	South East Asia Treaty Organisation
START (1 & 2)	Strategic Arms Reduction Talks
TVNZ	Television New Zealand
USIA	United States Information Agency
VTOL	Vertical Take Off and Landing (carrier)
WACL	World Anti-Communist League

Introduction

When David Lange led the New Zealand Labour Party to victory in the 1984 general election, the rest of the world took notice. After a decade on the Opposition benches, perhaps the election of a Labour government was remarkable enough, but it was the promise to ban nuclear-powered and/or -armed warships[1] from New Zealand ports, and to codify that ban in 'nuclear-free' legislation, which captured the world's attention.

In a country not noted for radical foreign policy or defence leanings the Labour pledge to ban nuclear warships pushed New Zealand to centre stage in the international political arena. Here was a country that rarely upset the status quo, poised to snub its nose at the nuclear navies of the United States and even its 'mother country' Britain. The governments of the United States, Britain and Australia were not impressed by New Zealand threatening to 'rock the boat'.

In this book we examine the attempts that were made during the first term of the Labour government from 1984 to 1987 to achieve a change of policy in New Zealand which would allow nuclear warship visits to continue.

The book comprises a specific case-study of the pressures that one state can (and did) exert on another in an attempt to bend it to its will. In the case of New Zealand and the United States, this had the added ingredient of being an unequal relationship, with the United States ostensibly having

1. Throughout this book frequent reference is made to the 'nuclear ships ban' and the 'ban on nuclear ships'. Unless otherwise stated, these references should be read as shorthand versions of the more cumbersome 'ban on nuclear-powered and/or -armed warships'. It may also be assumed that the terms cover 'nuclear-capable' warships too.

a far greater range in the forms and methods of pressure which it could use against New Zealand. In fact this exaggerated imbalance of power could easily have worked against the United States who, as it will become clear in this book, had to be wary of creating the impression of threatening a weaker nation.

Because this book focuses primarily on the New Zealand/United States relationship, there is less concentration on the role of New Zealand in the Australia, New Zealand, United States (ANZUS) alliance.[2] Other books have concentrated on the evolution of this alliance, and on the obligations and rights which extend to its three members.[3] What we are concerned with here is presenting a case-study of three years of intensive pressures designed to reverse a foreign policy decision arrived at by a newly-elected New Zealand government.

In the first chapter the decision taken by the Labour government of 1984 to ban nuclear warships from New Zealand is placed in an historical context by an examination of the geographical isolation of New Zealand and the development of the country's foreign policy from its colonial days, and by consideration of the fact that the Labour Party had long had a thread of idealism and an internationalist foreign policy outlook within it. The chapter also spends some time tracing the development of social protest movements of the 1970s and '80s which were a powerful political lobby in the country at the time of the 1984 election.

In the following chapter the 1984 'snap' general election is described. Of particular relevance was the fact that the election was called by the Prime Minister Robert Muldoon ostensibly because he could not guarantee a majority in Parliament after one of his MPs declared that she would cross the floor and support a Bill banning nuclear warships from New Zealand's ports. The nuclear issue was prominent in the election campaign and was watched closely by commentators around the world.

With the Labour Party sweeping to power, the scene was set for a confrontation between the members of the ANZUS alliance which arguably had formed the hub of the western alliance in the South Pacific. The implicit/explicit nuclear or non-nuclear nature of the ANZUS Treaty was a debate which was to continue during the years following the Labour

2. For the text of the ANZUS Treaty see the Appendix to this volume, pp. 173–5 below.
3. See, for example, Jacob Bercowitch (ed.), *ANZUS in Crisis: Alliance Management in International Affairs*, Macmillan, London, 1988, and Stuart McMillan, *Neither Confirm Nor Deny – The nuclear ships dispute between New Zealand and the United States*, Allen & Unwin/Port Nicholson Press, 1987.

government's election. But whatever the outcome of that debate, the fact would remain that the United States, Britain and Australia were keen to see the nuclear ships ban reversed. And of these three countries, the United States was the most explicit in its denunciation of the Lange government's nuclear-free policies.

Since the main body of this book comprises a case-study of the ways in which the United States in particular attempted to undermine and ultimately reverse the ships-ban, it is necessary to establish two things. Firstly, exactly why the United States found New Zealand's policy so offensive, and secondly, what options were available to the US in their attempts to overturn the ban. This is examined in Chapters 3 and 4. In Chapter 3, the US concern with events in New Zealand is placed in the context of developments in US foreign policy, and in particular the 'rearming of America' under the Reagan administration, which included the deployment of new intermediate-range nuclear weapons in Western Europe, and the development of a more aggressive maritime strategy. Clearly such developments were not aided by the actions of a previously trusted ally which was taking steps to remove itself from the nuclear infrastructure of the West. In Chapter 4 we examine the methods of persuasion which were available to the United States in its attempts to reverse the ships-ban, or at least find a compromise which would allow the visits of US warships to continue. Not all of these would be applicable to the New Zealand 'problem'. Direct military intervention, for example, was never an option to be considered, but diplomatic and political pressures, propaganda campaigns, economic threats and even covert operations were all plausible tactics in attempting to reverse the New Zealand policy.

Having established the background to the decision to ban nuclear warships from New Zealand's territorial waters, and the reasons why this was met with consternation in Washington, London and Canberra, Chapters 5 to 9 take the form of a chronology of events and actions throughout the first term of the government until the general election of August 1987.

Chapter 5 describes the first six months of the Labour government – a time when no request for port facilities was made by Britain or the United States. However these months gave a foretaste of the kinds of pressure and retaliation which could be expected from the United States if the ships-ban was implemented by the Labour government. In some respects, the first six months set the pattern for the rest of the dispute.

After this period, the first request for port facilities in New Zealand was made by the United States. In Chapter 6 this request – and subsequent refusal – is described in detail. Following the refusal to allow an American warship to dock at a New Zealand port, the attempts to reverse the ships-ban intensified during the following two months of February and March 1985. Diplomatic, military, economic, trade, media and domestic political pressures to rescind the ban put an intense strain on the Lange government and these multi-faceted attempts are the subject of a detailed description in Chapter 7.

Chapter 8 charts further developments in the dispute throughout the following twenty-one months of sustained pressure. A new US ambassador was appointed to Wellington; the Greenpeace flagship *Rainbow Warrior* was bombed and sunk in Auckland harbour; David Lange became more defensive of the nuclear-free policies, and the government introduced legislation to codify the ban in law; the United States withdrew its 'security guarantee' to New Zealand and there were examples of suspected covert attempts to undermine the ban. These are just a few of the events which kept the ANZUS dispute in the headlines during 1985 and 1986.

In Chapter 9 we examine how the pressures on New Zealand to rescind the ships-ban were resisted as the country geared up for its general election in August 1987. Again, the attempts to achieve a change in the policy on nuclear ships were fought on several fronts, but to little avail. When the election campaign began, the Labour government seemed to have an unassailable lead in the polls. As the weeks passed, this lead was rapidly whittled away, and for many observers it was only their nuclear-free policies which won Labour a second term of government.

With the Labour government re-elected, and the nuclear-free policy enshrined in New Zealand law, it would appear that the United States, Britain and Australia failed totally in their attempts to overturn the ships-ban. In the concluding chapter to this book we discuss the issues that the ban raised, and analyse the success or failure of the pressures to undermine and ultimately overturn it. We discuss, too, the international ramifications of the 'New Zealand example'; the possible influence that the ships-ban had on some NATO countries, and the reasons why it was, and remains, such a popular domestic policy in New Zealand. This final chapter also discusses the limitations of the New Zealand ships-ban and addresses the arguments which claim that attempting to disengage from participation in a nuclear strategy whilst remaining in an alliance such as ANZUS is ultimately a contradictory and perhaps untenable policy. With this in mind, we offer some tentative suggestions as to what steps New

Zealand could now take to reinforce the nuclear-free policies it has followed, and in so doing establish itself as a true 'peacemaker' in the Pacific.

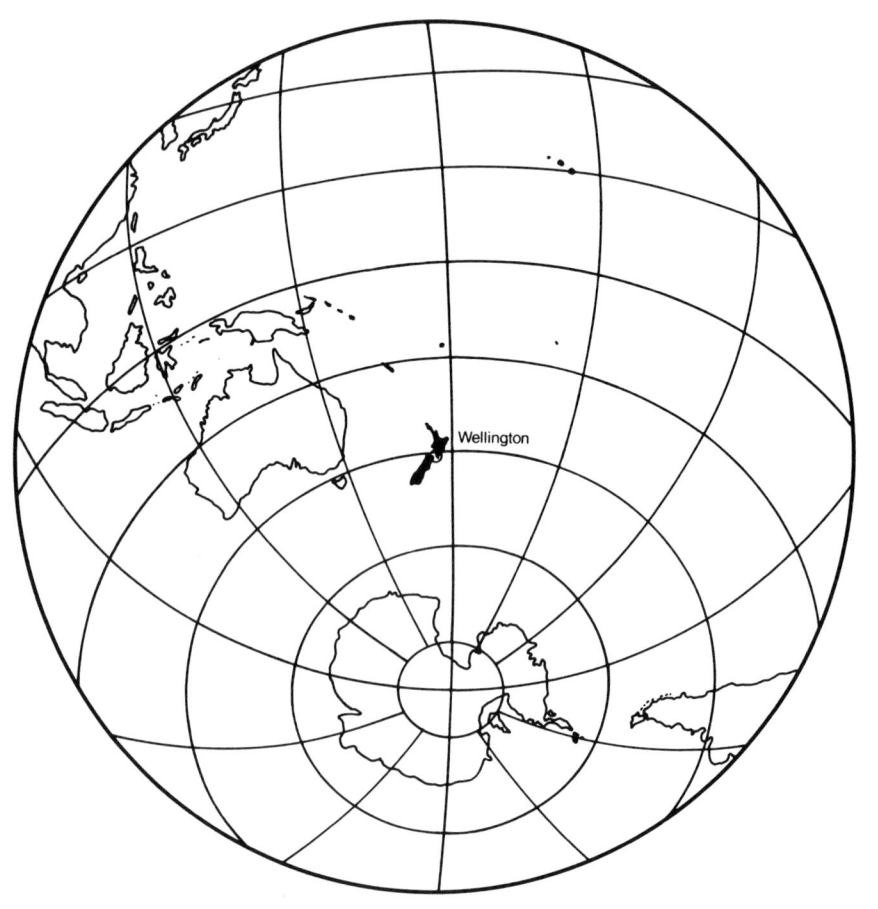

The World from New Zealand

CHAPTER 1

Setting the Context: Geography, Foreign Policy and Protest

The main body of this book concerns itself with the attempts during the first term of the 1984 Labour government to overturn the ban on nuclear-powered and nuclear-armed warships from New Zealand ports. However, the ban needs to be placed in some sort of historical and geographical context for its true significance to be realised. Accordingly, in this chapter we will look briefly at four main elements in the evolution of New Zealand's nuclear-free policies of 1984.

Firstly, the geographical location of New Zealand will be briefly discussed. Secondly, there will be an historical overview of the development of New Zealand's foreign policy from its colonial days to the present. Then, a similar examination of the Labour Party's tradition in foreign policy. And finally, there will be a brief examination of social protest movements in the country, and particularly the contemporary peace movement which was so influential in achieving the nuclear ships ban policy.

Lying in the South West Pacific, New Zealand is 1,600 kilometres from the East coast of Australia, over 2,500 kilometres from New Caledonia (Kanaky), Fiji, Vanuatu, Tonga and Samoa, and 10,000 kilometres from both Japan and the West coast of the United States of America.[1]

1. Figures taken from Kevin Clements, 'New Zealand's Relations with the UK, the US and the Pacific', *Alternatives* (New York), vol. 14, winter 1986, pp. 595f.

The map opening this chapter shows the boundary of the earth's hemisphere centred on New Zealand's capital city Wellington. It strikingly illustrates the enormity of the Pacific basin which is rimmed by both the United States and the Soviet Union, Nicaragua, Korea, the Philippines, Chile and Japan among others. The Pacific Basin constitutes almost one half of the globe, and New Zealand lies close to the middle of it – surrounded by the world's largest moat. Perhaps a more graphic illustration of the size of the Pacific is the fact that, flying from Britain, it takes approximately twelve hours to reach the West coast of the United States, and the edge of the Pacific. But at this point you are only halfway to New Zealand – another twelve hours flying time, and all of it over the Pacific Ocean.[2] These facts should constantly be borne in mind when reading this book, for a great many of the arguments in support of the nuclear ships ban cite New Zealand's geographical isolation as its greatest 'defence'. In contrast, the extent of the reaction by the United States to the ban might seem initially surprising in view of the relatively minor significance of New Zealand's strategic importance to the United States.

Turning to the country itself, a few figures will be helpful. It is 1,600 kilometres in length and consists of three main islands. The two major ones are the North (114,829 square kilometres) and the South (153,979 square kilometres), with the third, Stewart Island (1,700 square kilometres), lying directly south of the South Island. As of 31 March 1985, the population was 3.2 million – roughly equivalent to that of West Yorkshire in Britain.[3] The colonial history of New Zealand will be familiar to most readers, and there is not space here to outline that history, although it should be noted that the nuclear ships ban is in many ways synonymous with the break from a colonial economic and military dependency.

New Zealand Foreign Policy: An Historical Overview

When New Zealand first looked at the world, it did so secure in the knowledge that its security lay in the hands of the Royal Navy, and its economy protected by the British marketplace. As a remote dependency of the British Empire, New Zealand was more concerned with supporting

2. From Owen Wilkes, 'Nuclearisation and Militarisation of the Pacific', *Sanity*, August 1987, pp. 15–17.
3. Population figures cited in *1986 Air New Zealand Almanac*, Moa Almanac Press, Auckland, 1985.

British foreign policy than with the advancement of its own specific national interests.

The last British troops withdrew from New Zealand in 1870, but when New Zealand troops first went overseas to fight for Britain in the Transvaal in 1899, Prime Minister Richard Seddin still felt able to declare: 'The British flag is our protection. . . . In prosperity we share, in adversity likewise, we will not shrink from our share of the responsibility.'[4] Similarly, on 4 September 1939 New Zealand Prime Minister Michael Savage broadcast to the nation the now legendary remarks: 'Both with gratitude for the past and with confidence in the future, we range ourselves without fear beside Britain. Where she goes, we go, where she stands, we stand.'[5] Indeed, during the twentieth century New Zealanders have fought and died on the battlegrounds of Africa (during the Boer War), Europe (through two world wars), the Middle East and the Pacific (in the Second World War) and Asia (in Korea; during the Malaya emergency; in Indonesia; and in Vietnam). As John Henderson poignantly remarks: 'If in some future century, an archaeologist uncovers a New Zealand war memorial, he may be forgiven for concluding that during the Twentieth Century New Zealand had attained great power status.'[6] The truth, however, is that historically New Zealand's 'enemies' have always been those of its great power allies. Such a willingness to fight in distant lands in someone else's war can best be explained in terms of an 'insurance policy' reasoning. For as New Zealand's security depended upon the power and influence of its major ally (initially Britain, but later the USA), it was in its self-interest to pay its premium and provide military assistance when required.

For New Zealand, the urgency of the fight against fascism and Nazism in the Second World War was subsequently overshadowed in 1942 with the fall of Singapore – and the collapse of British power in the Pacific. This led to a re-appraisal of New Zealand's then total dependence on Britain for defence. New Zealand and Australia, with most of their armed forces absent in the Middle East, perceived a threat of Japanese invasion and became dependent for their immediate military security on United States forces in the Pacific.

---

4. Quoted in Charles Osborne (ed.), *Australia, New Zealand and the South Pacific – A Handbook*, Anthony Blond Ltd, London, 1970, p. 360.
5. Cited in Les Cleveland, *Government and Politics in New Zealand*, School of Political Science and Public Administration, Victoria University Press, Wellington, 1978, p. 231.
6. John Henderson et al., *Beyond New Zealand: The Foreign Policy of a Small State*, Reed Methuen, Auckland, 1980, p. 3.

This shift in the balance of power in the Pacific away from Britain to the United States determined the subsequent course of New Zealand foreign policy. Initially, there was an assumption that the 'special relationship' which had developed during the Second World War between the US and Britain would continue, but the rapid dissolution of allied wartime alliances was matched by the diversity of interest between Britain and the United States. This led to successive New Zealand governments attempting to 'please' both nations – although scarcely concealing that a major objective was to cultivate the best and closest possible relations with the US (who had fond memories of the commitment and sacrifice made by New Zealand during the war).

By the 1950s New Zealand was looking to the United States as the ultimate guarantor of its security, whilst continuing to regard Britain as a partner in defence and trade. This shift in focus was fortified by the signing of the ANZUS Treaty in September 1951.

The signing of the Treaty formed part of a process of adjustment by New Zealand to what was a fundamentally new security situation. British interests in the Pacific area were contracting with the demise of the colonial empire, whereas New Zealand was beginning to see its future as being increasingly bound up with Asia and the Pacific rather than Europe. And at the same time as these changes in the strategic sphere were occurring, changes in the economic sphere were looming large on the horizon too.

At the end of the Second World War, New Zealand's pattern of trade had revealed an almost exclusive relationship with the UK. New Zealand supplied raw materials and the UK supplied manufactured goods. Because of the small size of New Zealand's population this pattern was mutually beneficial – allowing the development of an advanced (and in many ways pioneering) welfare state in New Zealand upon a predominantly agricultural base. However, the concentration upon a single trading partner for both imports and exports, the limited range of commodities, and the heavy financial reliance upon Britain meant that the New Zealand economy had an extremely narrow base.

The dangers of such a narrow economy were exposed in the years following the Second World War when the erosion of British economic strength meant that the country was unable to provide a market for all of New Zealand's exports, or an adequate source of investment capital which New Zealand needed for its economic growth. It was perhaps this uncomfortable reality which led for the first time to a direct correlation in public consciousness between domestic and external issues in the formulation of New Zealand foreign policy.

Several writers have broken down the evolution of New Zealand's foreign policy into distinct periods. For J.S. Hoadley there are three such periods which he labels as Commonwealth, American and National Independence. Keith Jackson chooses four distinctive periods of evolution, and these provide a succinct analysis of New Zealand foreign policy.[7]

We have already seen that in the immediate aftermath of the Second World War New Zealand continued to hold a Euro-centric view of world affairs. The fall of Singapore and decline of the British Empire were fundamental in sowing the seeds of doubt and change, but it was the Suez Crisis of 1956 which precipitated the search for a new identity in New Zealand. Suez posed a difficult choice for New Zealand arising from a major disagreement between Britain and the USA over the legitimacy of the British action. The strong historical and cultural ties with Britain were enough to warrant New Zealand support, but the real significance of Suez was that it marked the end of an era. Henceforth the US was to be in all practical purposes the primary 'protector' of New Zealand in matters of defence. Jackson sees this period from the Second World War to 1956 as the first stage of New Zealand's evolution to an independent foreign policy.[8]

Following Suez up until 1972, Jackson believes New Zealand was engaged in a search for its own identity. On the one hand, the country was firmly drawn into the US sphere of influence (best expressed in the controversial commitment of New Zealand troops to fight in Vietnam), and on the other hand, Britain's intention in 1962 to apply for membership of the European Community in effect signalled the beginning of the end of New Zealand's unhindered access to the British marketplace. As M. Norrish writes: 'We [New Zealand] didn't run away from home, home ran away from us. Britain joined the European Community; and by that action forced New Zealand to seek new markets.'[9] This fundamental change in the economic relationship with Britain meant that New Zealand had to rely heavily on economic diplomacy to find new markets for its exports, and on the United States to provide it with international credit.

7. J.S. Hoadley, 'The Future of New Zealand's Alliances', *New Zealand International Review*, vol. IX, no. 6, Nov./Dec. 1984, p. 6. Keith Jackson, 'Attitudes and Alliances 1945–76', in Henderson et al., *Beyond New Zealand*, pp. 16–22.
8. Jackson, 'Attitudes and Alliances 1945–76', pp. 16–22.
9. M. Norrish, 'The Changing Context of New Zealand's Foreign Policy', *The Australian Quarterly*, vol. 58, no. 2, winter 1986, pp. 192–7.

The third period in the evolution of New Zealand foreign policy is, in Jackson's opinion, from 1972 to 1975. At this time the effect of loosening ties with Britain (or more accurately Britain loosening ties with New Zealand) led to an increase of aspirations for independence in New Zealand. This was reflected in the election of a Labour government in 1972 which promised a greater self-reliance and independence coupled with an internationalist approach to foreign affairs.

New Zealand had arrived at a watershed: 'The storm warnings of 1960–61 about British entry into the EEC had grown to a loud roar and the question became a major national preoccupation. . . . The seeming intractability of the situation in Vietnam gave rise to public questioning of the country's whole relationship with the US. . . . Even the validity of the ANZUS relationship was called into question.'[10]

French nuclear testing in the Pacific – with US support – provoked an uproar and an increased awareness of New Zealand's growing involvement with the newly independent nation-states of the South Pacific. However, the high hopes that New Zealand was on the threshold of a genuinely independent status in foreign policy were short-lived. This was principally due to a disastrous downturn in the New Zealand economy which saw a balance of payments surplus of NZ$130m in June 1972 become a deficit of NZ$1067m in just three years.[11] As Jackson notes: 'It is clearly difficult to indulge a new found feeling of independence in the face of rapidly mounting debts.'[12] Largely as a result of this enormous balance of payments deficit, the traditional view that New Zealand simply could not afford the luxury of 'independent' views in foreign policy quickly resurfaced, even if the economic downturn had been due, in large part, to circumstances beyond New Zealand's control, especially the 1973–4 oil price rises by the Organisation of Petroleum Exporting Countries' (OPEC) member states.

Jackson sees the period from 1975 onwards as being one of 'qualified dependence'. The pressing need to find new markets led New Zealand to increase its emphasis on resource diplomacy. That is, New Zealand used fishing rights in its waters as a bargaining chip for trade rights – principally with Japan. The development of relations with South Pacific states, through such organisations as the Pacific Forum, helped to foster indepen-

10. George Laking, 'The Evolution of an Independent Foreign Policy', in Henderson et al., *Beyond New Zealand*, p. 15.
11. Jackson, 'Attitudes and Alliances 1945–76', p. 21.
12. Ibid.

dence ideas, and more recently the Closer Economic Relations (CER) agreement with Australia has opened up the potential for more trade links across the Tasman.

In summary, we have seen that in some measure by choice, but more so due to the changes in the international environment, New Zealand governments were forced to develop their own independent responses to world affairs. This change, though far from complete, stemmed from the realisation that the economic and strategic interests of the industrialised western nations and those of a small isolated Pacific island country did not necessarily coincide. Certainly New Zealand governments of both political colours have contributed to this growing independent outlook, but it is the Labour Party alone which has always been characterised, to an extent at least, by an independent, outward-looking and international-ist foreign policy. Conversely, the National Party (and before them the United and Reform parties) have accepted the dominant western percep-tions of where New Zealand's interests lie unless and until external politics have forced them to alter their foreign policy direction.

Labour and Foreign Policy

The Labour Party in New Zealand has been in power for little more than twenty years in the last half century. When David Lange took the party to victory in the July 1984 general election he led only the fourth Labour government in New Zealand's history.

The following brief examination of the three previous Labour govern-ments' foreign policy initiatives is useful because it illustrates that there has been a continuum of an outward-looking, and in some measure independent foreign policy in them all. This is perhaps most apparent in the 1972 Kirk/Rowling government, but it begins with the first Labour government which came to power in 1935 and remained in office until 1949.

The Labour Party was steeped in anti-militarism, anti-imperialism and internationalism, so it was no surprise that the Labour government of Michael J. Savage placed a high priority on support for the League of Nations. It was in this forum that the government publicly and vocifer-ously disagreed with Britain over the Spanish Civil War, and later criticised the British policy of appeasement. Furthermore, British recog-nition of the Italian regime in Ethiopia (1938) and the Franco regime in

13

Spain (1939) was not echoed by New Zealand.[13]

During the Second World War the New Zealand government (a wartime administration between 30 June 1942 and 2 October 1942) supported the British with men and supplies, but in retrospect the war also served to mature New Zealand's approach to international affairs. Savage realised that, with the demise of British colonial power, New Zealand needed a voice in Washington as well as in London.

In 1940 Savage died and was succeeded by Peter Fraser. Through the concept of collective security, Fraser sought to give the small nations of the world a greater voice. His government also opened diplomatic posts in the Soviet Union and Canada and in 1943 established the Department of External Affairs. Labour worked closely with the newly formed United Nations, and Fraser became an outstanding international leader championing the causes of the small nations against those of the larger powers. However, the decision by Fraser to send (conscripted) New Zealand troops to support the British in the Middle East in 1949 met with much criticism and the charge that Labour's anti-militarism and internationalism had given way to anti-communism.[14]

Labour lost power in 1949 and the subsequent eight year reign of the National Party saw the Japanese Peace Treaty, the ANZUS alliance and the South East Asia Treaty Organisation (SEATO) come into being, as well as the abortive Anglo-French invasion of Suez (with New Zealand support).[15] The second Labour government, elected in 1957, was led by Walter Nash, who had a greater experience in foreign affairs than any previous Prime Minister. During a period when the first Cold War was at its peak, his receptivity to the ideas of neutralism and non-alignment was in stark contrast to the conventional foreign policy wisdom of the day. He passionately believed that the small nations had a role to play: 'Cannot [they] . . . do something to break this deadlock and bring about a new approach towards peace through disarmament?'[16]

In other areas, such as nuclear testing, it must be said that Nash was more equivocal – even to the point of supplying two New Zealand frigates as weather ships during British tests at Christmas Island. Moreover, his backing for sporting links with South Africa did little to gain him support

13. See W.D. McIntyre, 'Labour Experience in Foreign Policy', in Hyam Gold (ed.), *New Directions In New Zealand Foreign Policy*, Benton Ross, Auckland, 1985, pp. 11–15.
14. Ibid., p. 19.
15. See Jackson, 'Attitudes and Alliances 1945–76', pp. 16–22.
16. Cited in McIntyre, 'Labour Experience in Foreign Policy', p. 20.

14

in the black African countries. In 1960 Nash defended the right of the New Zealand All Blacks Rugby Union side to tour South Africa, whilst simultaneously denouncing the evils of apartheid. The arguments that sport and politics are separate/inseparable were to return to prominence in later years under a National government.

After just three years in office, Labour were defeated in the general election of 1960 and had to wait for over a decade before returning to power in 1972 under Norman Kirk's premiership. This new Labour government signalled a radical breakaway from the conservative foreign policy of the preceding National administration. In the wake of the Vietnam debacle there was a resurgence of anti-militarism and internationalism in New Zealand, which was matched by Kirk's belief that foreign policy should be based on moral principles.

Kirk called for a more effective voice for small states in disarmament negotiations, urged a United Nations conference to see through the proposed Comprehensive Test Ban Treaty, supported a zone for peace in the Indian Ocean and promised close consultation with New Zealand's Pacific neighbours over the establishment of a Nuclear Weapon Free Zone (NWFZ) in the South Pacific.[17] In addition, the Kirk years saw the last New Zealand troops withdrawn from Vietnam, the Peoples Republic of China officially recognised, the New Zealand Embassy in Moscow re-opened (it had been closed by the National government), a proposed South African *Springbok* rugby tour of New Zealand banned, and proceedings begun in the International Court of Justice against French nuclear testing in the Pacific. A New Zealand frigate sent as a 'silent accusing witness' to the French nuclear weapon test site at Mururoa gained unprecedented international media coverage.[18]

Perhaps more significantly, in the light of recent experience, the Labour government also banned nuclear-powered warships from New Zealand's ports. By 1975 the ban was under considerable strain as the United States government made requests for port visits by its nuclear-powered and -armed warships. Norman Kirk had died in office in 1974, and Wallace Rowling took over the leadership for the year that remained prior to the next scheduled general election. Like Kirk, Rowling took a healthy (some

17. See Rod Alley, 'Disarmament and New Zealand Foreign Policy', in Henderson et al., *Beyond New Zealand*, p. 113.
18. Several writers cover in some detail the years of the Third Labour government. For example see: Alley 'Disarmament and New Zealand Foreign Policy', pp. 111–16; Cleveland, *Government and Politics in New Zealand* (esp. pp. 231–9); and McIntyre, 'Labour Experience in Foreign Policy', pp. 22–5.

would argue excessive) interest in foreign affairs, perhaps to the neglect of the domestic issues that were to cost the Labour government the next election. The United States used the Whitlam government in Australia to lean on New Zealand, and on 10 July 1975 Rowling announced that the New Zealand government was 're-examining its policy of not permitting nuclear powered ships to call at New Zealand ports, but at the moment there are no plans for change'.[19]

In essence, under Kirk and Rowling, New Zealand sought a strategy of qualified alignment – never breaking ties with traditional allies – but nevertheless prepared to dissent from policies they found repugnant. They did this by relying on moral and symbolic, rather than military, force to advance their argument. According to Cleveland: 'The protestations of "independence" made by Kirk and his assertion that principles of morality ought to guide the views of small nations like New Zealand. . . . were careful gestures in the direction of a slightly more autonomous foreign policy.'[20]

The attempts by Kirk and Rowling to guide New Zealand towards a greater independence in foreign affairs abruptly ceased with the return of a National government in 1975. The Kirk government was badly hit by the oil crisis of 1973 and had fallen short of its high economic promises and expectations. American support for the National Party opposition had been no secret, and the US was ultimately rewarded by New Zealand's return to a total and seemingly unquestioning foreign policy alignment. New Zealand Prime Minister Robert Muldoon immediately opened New Zealand ports to US nuclear warships again, and a more sceptical attitude towards the proposals for a South Pacific Nuclear Free Zone ensued.[21]

Despite the various ambiguities, equivocations and the overall foreign policy alignment with the West, there has been a common thread running through all three Labour governments which has had at its core an internationalist, anti-militarist philosophy. According to W.D. McIntyre, the early attitudes of anti-imperialism and anti-militarism have been recently manifested in the anti-nuclear and anti-apartheid beliefs of the party.[22] And speaking at the 1984 Labour Party Victory Conference, the then President of the party, Jim Anderton, said: 'The policies of 1917, in

19. Cited in Tom Newnham, *Peace Squadron – The Sharp End of Nuclear Protest in New Zealand*, Graphic Publications, Auckland, 1986. p. 8.
20. Cleveland, *Government and Politics in New Zealand*, p. 235.
21. See Alley, 'Disarmament and New Zealand Foreign Policy', p. 113.
22. McIntyre, 'Labour Experience in Foreign Policy', p. 25.

16

principle, are the policies we espouse today. The anti-war sentiment of 1918 which embodies the Labour philosophy that war offers no solution to national or international problems is the same principle on which the Labour Party opposes nuclear weapons and their proliferation in 1984.'[23]

But it is open to debate how great the nuclear-free commitment of the Labour Party would have been in 1984 had it not been for a powerful peace movement which at a grassroots level had built up tremendous support for a 'nuclear-free New Zealand'. In the final part of this chapter it will be interesting to look briefly at the background of this peace movement, and at the ways in which it captured world attention and public support.

Protest Movements in New Zealand

Pressure and protest groups have been active in New Zealand politics since the nineteenth century. Initially, the church was a powerful lobby in the country and joined forces with the temperance movement in seeking to restrict the sale of alcohol and tighten licensing laws. There followed movements for social change concerned with the broad spectrum of issues and campaigns associated with most democracies. From women's rights to animal welfare, from civil liberties to censorship, New Zealand has a history of spontaneous protest and public campaigning.

Environmental conservation was a politically sensitive issue in the 1970s and has continued to be so, but in the early protests 'extreme' actions, such as civil disobedience, were avoided and laws not broken.

However, of particular interest and of most relevance to this book are the early anti-war and anti-apartheid protests in New Zealand which were the immediate predecessors of the current peace movement.

The protests against the Vietnam War were not so restrained as the earlier environmental demonstrations. Committees on Vietnam were formed to protest against the involvement of New Zealand troops in the war, the continuation of the war itself and visits by US politicians and military officers. There were mass rallies, protest marches and silent vigils. As the war continued, the protests became more turbulent and disruptive with violent clashes between the police and demonstrators. Les Cleveland believes that the New Zealand protesters may have been

23. Jim Anderton, *New Zealand Labour Party: Report of the Victory Conference (President's Report)*, Wellington, 7–10 September 1984, New Zealand Labour Party, Wellington, 1984, p. 7.

responding to, and imitating, similar demonstrations in the United States and Britain.[24] He even goes as far as to suggest that the '[history] of protest and demonstration in New Zealand can be seen as a by-product of the television era, which has not only facilitated the conversion of politics into instant theatre but has also introduced visual images of violent global conflict into ordinary living rooms in a readily assimilable, informative and repetitive way.'[25]

Such a view might be a discredit to the integrity and intelligence of the New Zealand protesters and it certainly ignores the fact that protest movements were not simply a phenomenon of the 1960s but predated the advent of television. However, there is some truth in the notion that the global news media has facilitated the need for eye-catching 'newsworthy' protests.

In addition to protests against the Vietnam War, since the 1960s ideological conflict in New Zealand has deepened over the problems of environmental change, nuclear testing in the Pacific, the deployment of nuclear weapons in New Zealand waters, and the readiness of New Zealand governments to allow sporting contacts with South Africa.

Two umbrella organisations were at the forefront of the campaigns to stop sporting contacts with South Africa. The Halt All Racist Tours (HART) organisation and the Citizens' Association for Racial Equality (CARE) built up a prolonged campaign against such sporting contacts. This came to a head in 1981 when the anti-apartheid movement staged massive demonstrations at fixtures involving a visiting South African *Springbok* team. According to Geoff Chapple, the tour had been set up with 'encouragement from the Police and a singular absence of government pressure against it'.[26]

The mobilisation of opposition to the tour involved large-scale civil disobedience and direct action in an attempt (successful in some cases) to prevent the rugby matches being played. The response of the government was not to stop the tour in the interests of civic order but to turn the issue into one of law and order and the 'right' of people to play sport with whomever they wish. The violence of the specially trained police squads against protesters would have been hard to believe had it not been

---

24. Les Cleveland, 'The Sound and the Fury: Ideologically Motivated Pressure Groups', in Gold (ed.), *New Zealand Politics in Perspective*, Longman Paul, Takapuna, Auckland, 1985, p. 234.
25. Ibid., p. 236.
26. Geoff Chapple, *1981: The Tour*, A.H. & A.W. Reed, Wellington, 1984, p. 30.

captured on news film, and shown around the world.[27]

The tour gave a very high profile to foreign policy issues and led to intense debate about New Zealand's role in the world. According to Kevin Clements:

> The ramifications were extensive, dividing New Zealand in ways that would have been considered impossible before the South Africans arrived in the country. . . . It confronted the indigenous people of New Zealand with problems of racism and independence leading the Maori/ Pacific island groups within New Zealand to assess their links with independence movements in the Pacific and their involvement in the sustained opposition to French nuclear testing.[28]

The violence and widespread protests surrounding the 1981 *Springbok* tour have been interpreted as signalling the collapse of traditional consensus-finding politics in New Zealand and heralding the emergence of a more divisive style of leadership.

Parallel to, and in some cases overlapping the protests against Vietnam and the *Springbok* tour, was the emergence of a strong peace movement in the country. Vietnam had led many to question New Zealand's military involvement with the United States and in particular the participation in US nuclear strategy in the South Pacific. Student protests in the 1960s sought the removal of US military bases in New Zealand, and in June 1968 they were successful in persuading the government to oppose the construction of an OMEGA naval transmitter in the Southern Alps of the South Island. OMEGA was to be a Very Low Frequency radio transmitter for submarine communication. Speculation grew that OMEGA would be used by Polaris nuclear-armed submarines for the accurate positioning they would need to launch nuclear missiles. After three years of widespread protests, the United States, despite the fact that New Zealand was a superior site technically, decided to build the transmitter in Australia, where they believed the political climate would be more favourable towards the base.[29]

27. For a detailed account of the protests in New Zealand against the 1981 South African *Springbok* tour see ibid.
28. Clements, 'New Zealand's Relations with the UK, the US and the Pacific', pp. 595–6.
29. The controversy surrounding the OMEGA base and other US bases in New Zealand is detailed in Owen Wilke's book *Protest*, Alister Taylor, Wellington, 1973. See also Bob Leonard, 'United States Military Bases and Projects in New Zealand', in Barbara Harford (ed.), *Beyond ANZUS – Alternatives for Australia, New Zealand and the Pacific*, Beyond ANZUS Committee Peace Movement Aotearoa, Wellington, 1985.

From the 1960s to the present day the New Zealand peace movement has consistently maintained that the country's involvement in ANZUS, its willingness to provide port facilities for US warships and its involvement in US military exercises affords more insecurity than security in that it binds the country to the US nuclear infrastructure hence making New Zealand a potential target in a nuclear war.

By the 1970s the peace issue began to figure prominently in New Zealand's domestic politics. With the election of a Labour government in 1972, New Zealand began to adopt a more independent foreign policy and, as we saw earlier, banned nuclear-powered warships from its ports. When the incoming National government of 1975 indicated to the United States that their warships would once again be welcome in New Zealand ports, they seriously miscalculated the strength of feeling in the country against such visits. Future visits of United States warships and submarines were to be met by the 'Peace Squadron' – a flotilla of small boats, yachts and kayaks – which at great personal risk to their owners attempted physically to block the entry of the warships.[30] The land-based peace movement was also gaining momentum and seeking to make all of New Zealand a nuclear-free country.

By the late 1970s there existed in the country no bi-partisan consensus on foreign policy and defence issues. The Labour Party had passed resolutions at its conferences pledging to ban nuclear-powered and/or -armed warships from New Zealand ports, whilst the National government continued actively to encourage the warship visits. It has been suggested that then Prime Minister Robert Muldoon specifically requested the United States to send warships to New Zealand whereas the Americans, it seems, were keen to play down the visits for fear that they were creating an anti-American nationalist sentiment in New Zealand.

In 1981 an umbrella peace organisation was formed to help coordinate and link together the mushrooming peace movement. Peace Movement New Zealand[31] provides a national focus for the peace movement and is a resource and research base which has played a crucial role in raising public consciousness and keeping the government of the day under close scrutiny.

30. For a more detailed study of the 'Peace Squadron' movement in New Zealand see Newnham, *Peace Squadron*.
31. Aotearoa – 'Land of the Long White Cloud' – is the original Maori name for what most people now know as New Zealand. In recognition of, and support for, the struggle against colonialism by the Maori, Peace Movement New Zealand was later renamed Peace Movement Aotearoa.

Also in 1981 the New Zealand Nuclear Free Zone Committee (NZNFZC) was established. The Committee campaigned the length and breadth of the country in an attempt to persuade local councils to declare their municipalities as nuclear-free zones. The campaign met with impressive success: by 1 June 1984, over 61 per cent of all New Zealanders lived in locally declared nuclear-free zones,[32] and by October 1987 the figure had reached over 72 per cent.[33]

Together with these developments, the New Zealand women's movement had been taking an active interest in peace and disarmament issues. The visit of Dr Helen Caldicott on a speaking tour of the country engendered a much sharper opposition to nuclear weapons and the militarisation and colonialism of the Pacific. The women's protests at Greenham Common in Britain also served as an inspiration to the movement in New Zealand. Caldicott's visit also provided the catalyst for a dramatic expansion of 'professional' groups such as the International Physicians for the Prevention of Nuclear War, Scientists Against Nuclear Arms and the Medical Campaign Against Nuclear Weapons.

In political terms what had happened was that the peace movement had escaped from its left-wing shackles to become a broad-based movement which to some extent transcended class, race and party divisions. The National government was to pay a high price for ignoring this fact in the 1984 election.

This brief history of the protest/peace movement in New Zealand scarcely does credit to the strength and diversity of the imaginative campaigns that were waged. What it does illustrate is that the attempts at a much more independent foreign policy by past Labour governments – though in particular the Kirk/Rowling administration of 1972–5 were, in part at least, responses to a grassroots mood for change in New Zealand. External political and economic factors, whilst important, were not the only reason for changes in the perceptions and outlook. A well-informed and mobilised population in many ways dictated the pace and direction of this change.

---

32. Figures from *New Zealand Nuclear Free Zone Committee Newsletter* June/July 1984. Pub: NZNFZC, PO Box 18, 541 Christchurch, New Zealand.
33. Figures from *Nuclear Free*, The journal of the New Zealand Nuclear-Free Peacemaking Association (formerly the NZNFZC – as above) October 1987.

CHAPTER 2

The New Zealand General Election, 1984

At 11.15pm on Wednesday 13 June 1984, the New Zealand Prime Minister Sir Robert Muldoon announced that he could no longer be certain of a majority in Parliament and was therefore calling for its immediate dissolution.

What is of particular interest to this book is the fact that the calling of a 'snap' general election by Muldoon was precipitated, at least in part, by the threat of one of his MPs to cross the floor and vote with the Labour opposition in support of a bill banning nuclear weapons from New Zealand.

Marilyn Waring was elected a National MP in 1975 when she was still twenty-three years old. As a feminist, Waring never conformed to the National Party stereotype, and was not popular with Muldoon who patronisingly called her a 'very sad girl'.[1] In her autobiography Waring describes the process by which she came to refuse to support the government on the nuclear ships issue.[2] She declared that she would speak in favour of a 'nuclear-free' bill in 1982 but would vote against it if the government agreed to establish a Select Committee on Disarmament and Arms Control with wide terms of reference. 'I needed answers for myself: I didn't believe ANZUS obliged ship visits; I didn't believe there was a

1. Cited in Ged Martin, 'From Muldoon to Lange: New Zealand Votes in 1984', *The Round Table*, vol. 292 (1984), p. 395.
2. Marilyn Waring, *Women, Politics and Power* (Foreword by Robin Morgan), Allen & Unwin (NZ), Wellington, 1985.

Soviet build-up in the South Pacific; I was always aghast at the deterrence theory, and I wanted to know what the US installations in New Zealand did. . . . '[3]

The Select Committee was approved, but although it established New Zealand's right to prohibit nuclear warships from its ports, Muldoon continued to invite American warships to visit. In 1983 the USS *Texas* duly payed a port visit amid the growing demonstrations and attempts to blockade New Zealand's ports. Addressing the National Party's Annual Conference in Dunedin in July 1983, Marilyn Waring gave notice that her 'bottom line' was the exclusion of nuclear-capable ships from New Zealand's ports. Eleven months later both Waring and fellow National MP Mike Minogue voted with the Labour opposition for the 'Nuclear-Free New Zealand Bill' introduced to Parliament by Richard Prebble on 13 June 1984. It was only because two independent MPs counterbalanced these defections by voting with the government that Muldoon was able to hold on to his slender majority, and throw out the Bill.

In the following evening's Wellington-based *Evening Post* Minogue accused his government of 'increasingly unnacceptable arrogance' in throwing out the Bill. 'I think it's arrogance . . . that a government says in effect: "We don't need serious enquiry, we know best". I have never seen a question become so totally confused, whether by accident or design . . . '[4]

Despite the controversy surrounding the decision to throw out the nuclear-free Bill – and Marilyn Waring's subsequent decision to withdraw from the National Party caucus – there was little hint that Muldoon would call on the Governor-General to dissolve Parliament the following evening. In an attempt to resolve the issue a meeting was held on 14 June at which Robert Muldoon, Marilyn Waring, National Party President Sue Wood, director Barry Leay and the Chief Whip Don McKinnon were present. All attempts to dissuade Waring from withdrawing from the government caucus failed, and instead the Prime Minister called a special caucus meeting for 10.30pm the same evening after the New Zealand Parliament had risen. The meeting was quickly concluded with Robert Muldoon emerging from it to announce that he was visiting Government House immediately to arrange the dissolution of Parliament. The Governor-General, it seems, was caught out by the decision and hastily had to leave a dinner party to sign the proclamation.

---

3. Ibid., p. 113.
4. 'Defeat of Nuclear Bill "arrogance" says Minogue', *The Evening Post*, 14 June 1984.

According to the Prime Minister, he could no longer be certain of commanding a working majority in Parliament because of Marilyn Waring's withdrawal from the caucus. But the notion that Muldoon could no longer guarantee a parliamentary majority was not a convincing reason in itself for calling a 'snap' election. The National Party had been returned at the 1981 election with a majority of just two seats, but until 1984 Muldoon led the government as if it, and he, were invincible. Hence there was widespread speculation that he used the defection of Waring (who stressed that she would support the government on all matters except those relating to rape and nuclear weapons) as an excuse to exploit a favourable opportunity to go to the country. The economic indicators were good for the government with inflation down, unemployment dropping and productivity rising,[5] but were unlikely to remain so through to the scheduled time for the general election in November.

The Opposition were quick to exploit the situation by claiming that Muldoon was unable to present a budget to the country in existing circumstances and had chosen instead to look to any excuse for an early election in the hope that the short-term upturn in the economy would be sufficient to return him to office. There were good reasons to be concerned with the state of the economy. In 1979 the Muldoon government had undertaken to support many industries and the farming community with guaranteed prices and subsidies. At the same time, controls on overseas investment were relaxed and a new 'Think Big' economic policy followed. The 'Think Big' policy was based on the premise that New Zealand capital was not sufficient in itself to support widespread economic development. Hence the Muldoon government borrowed overseas capital on an unprecedented scale. The net external public debt for 1982–3 was US$6.9 billion,[6] a figure which gave New Zealand one of the highest levels of debt per capita. This increasing foreign debt put pressure on the value of the New Zealand dollar, while the increase in construction jobs which the 'Think Big' projects created were bound to be temporary. It is likely that Muldoon calculated that his government might have been able to win a July election, but would find it considerably more difficult were he to wait until November.

However, even if the Marilyn Waring and Mike Minogue 'defections'

5. See, for example, Keith Jackson, 'The New Zealand General Election of 1984', *Electoral Studies*, vol. 4, no. 1, April 1985, pp. 75–9.
6. Cited in Keith Suter, 'New Zealand's New Government', *Contemporary Review*, vol. 246, no. 1428, January, 1985, p. 2.

were an excuse rather than a reason for Muldoon calling a 'snap' election, they did serve to place the nuclear ships issue firmly on the election agenda and perhaps with a higher profile than might otherwise have been the case.

The 1984 general election was the first 'snap' election since 1951, and was significant also because it was fought with four nation-wide parties competing for power – something that had not occurred for fifty years. In addition to the National and Labour parties, the Social Credit Party (which had won over 20 per cent of the vote and two seats in the 1981 election) and the New Zealand Party fielded candidates in every seat.

The New Zealand Party was formed by Bob Jones, a millionaire business magnate and former friend of Sir Robert Muldoon. He had become disenchanted with National's economic policies and formed the New Zealand Party with the express purpose of putting an end to Muldoon's leadership.[7] With a neo-conservative philosophy, the party managed to combine right-wing opposition to economic controls with a left-wing radicalism including the decriminalisation of marijuana and a neutral foreign policy.[8] Although the party was only founded in 1983, it had rapidly grown in popularity and by 1984 was making a significant impression in the opinion polls.

The Social Credit Party had benefited from a widespread protest vote against Labour and National in the 1981 election, but had lost much credibility when its two MPs voted with the government on several contentious issues.[9] In particular, these MPs had saved the Muldoon government from defeat when they lent their support to legislation which enabled the government to build a huge dam in the South Island despite widespread criticism that the structure would result in the decimation of large areas of (increasingly rare) natural bush. The party did, however, advocate a defence policy based on armed neutrality and supported the call to ban nuclear warships from New Zealand ports. Nevertheless, Social Credit's role in the 1984 election was to be mainly defensive, and it lost many of its former supporters to the newly formed New Zealand Party.

At its 1984 conference, the Labour Party had the opportunity to pass a resolution calling for New Zealand's withdrawal from the ANZUS alliance. Instead it continued to support a policy which would ban all

---

7. See Alan Simpson, 'A New Generation Takes Over In New Zealand', *The Round Table*, vol. 299 (1986), p. 266.
8. Martin, 'From Muldoon to Lange', p. 395.
9. See Jackson, 'The New Zealand General Election of 1984', p. 76.

nuclear warships from New Zealand ports, but decided to remain in ANZUS. Thus three out of the four nation-wide political parties in New Zealand campaigned on anti-nuclear platforms. Only the National Party continued to espouse a policy of support for the continuation of visits by nuclear warships.

The hastily called election meant that the parties had very little time in which to compile comprehensive manifestos let alone conduct a pre-determined election campaign. Because of this, the campaign became dominated as much by personalities as by issues, if not more so. Robert Muldoon relied heavily on his past experience, and in particular his economic knowledge. He relied less on the actual record of the National government and instead spent time attacking the Labour Party leader's lack of experience in Parliament. In keeping with tradition, Muldoon also continued to allege communist infiltration of the trade unions and the Labour Party. He suffered, however, from a bitterness within the elec-torate to his abrasive leadership, and his nickname of 'Piggy Muldoon' was far from being an affectionate one. The tour of New Zealand by the South African *Springboks* in 1981 had polarised the country and the violent conflicts that the tour provoked were a legacy that was not forgotten. Similarly, the introduction of voluntary trade unionism had led to industrial unrest and the bombing of the Trades Hall in Wellington. Even National supporters recognised that Muldoon was possibly a liab-ility to the government's hopes of being re-elected. As the election cam-paign opened, opinion polls gave Labour a 46 per cent to 39 per cent lead over National.[10] By 29 June an opinion poll was putting Labour 12 per cent ahead, and comfortably heading for victory.[11]

The general election was held on 14 July 1984 and boasted a turn-out of 93.7 per cent of voters – the highest in fifty years.[12] A 4.2 per cent swing to Labour was sufficient for victory and a majority of 17 seats over National and Social Credit combined in Parliament. The Labour Party increased its share of the vote by 3.8 per cent whilst the National Party and Social Credit saw their votes fall by 2.9 per cent and 8 per cent respectively. With just 35.9 per cent of the total vote, the National Party recorded its lowest percentage in its history at a general election. The New Zealand Party, contesting its first general election, gained an impressive 12.4 per cent of the vote but no seats. Nevertheless, it could take comfort in the fact that it

10. Figures cited in Martin, 'From Muldoon to Lange', p. 397.
11. Ibid., p. 398.
12. Cited in Jackson, 'The New Zealand General Election of 1984', p. 76.

had achieved its primary aim of removing Muldoon from power. The Labour victory, then, needed to be seen in the context of a vote against National as much as a vote for Labour. New Zealand was ready for a change, and the Labour Party benefited from the tide of anti-Muldoonism which swept the country.

The Labour Party leader and new Prime Minister, David Lange, had entered Parliament in 1976. His background was as a Methodist lay preacher and a lawyer in Auckland with an impressive record of fighting for the underprivileged and powerless in New Zealand society.[13]

After being elected deputy leader of the Labour Party in 1979, Lange had failed by one vote a year later to take over the leadership from Bill Rowling. By late 1982, however, his popularity in the opinion polls had overtaken that of Rowling and when Rowling stood down on 3 February 1983, Lange took over the leadership. In his attacks on the National government, Lange concentrated on Muldoon's abrasive leadership and divisive politics, promising instead to get New Zealanders working together again, and promoting the Labour Party as the party of consensus.

At forty-one years old Lange was a young leader and represented a new influx of Labour MPs in the thirty to forty-five age group. This fact has since been used to explain Labour's new concern for 'efficiency' and 'professionalism' rather than an adherence to more traditional philosophies.[14]

The ANZUS row which erupted after Labour's ban on nuclear warships from New Zealand ports is discussed later. However, an early indication of the prominence which Lange gave to Labour's nuclear-free policies is contained in his address to the Labour Victory Conference less than two months after the general election:

> I venture that no incoming Government anywhere in the world has attributed the focus of attention of the people of the world by your saying through this Government that we absolutely abhor the nuclear arms race. . . . If you ever saw the response in mail that has come not just in New Zealand but throughout the world. . . . you would understand that your work and your striving were not in vain.[15]

13. The political career of David Lange is well charted by Vernon Wright in *David Lange – Prime Minister: A Profile By Vernon Wright*, Unwin Paperbacks with Port Nicholson Press, Wellington, 1984.
14. Simpson, 'A New Generation Takes Over', p. 267.
15. *New Zealand Labour Party: Report of Victory Conference*, Wellington, 7–10 September 1984, New Zealand Labour Party, Wellington, 1984. Address by the Prime Minister, Rt Hon. David Lange (9 Sept. 1984), p. 39

It was a speech which Lange both contradicted and re-affirmed more than once in the following years as he sought to spread the nuclear-free message and yet also deny that New Zealand's policies were to be seen as blueprints for other countries to follow.

CHAPTER 3

US Foreign Policy and the New Zealand Problem

When the Labour government led by David Lange was elected in 1984, the United States seemed unprepared for the challenge which Lange's anti-nuclear policies posed. It responded in a progressively firm manner, seeking to influence the New Zealand government itself as well as New Zealand public opinion.

For a powerful state such as the US there exists a wide variety of means to promote a foreign policy and, as we will see in Chapter 4, these include economic, diplomatic, military and other tactics. Elsewhere, in recent years, the United States has engaged in much stronger action to secure its objectives, but New Zealand represented a very different problem to those of Latin America, South East Asia or even the Middle East. Here, the cultural, linguistic and political links were strong, the country was a mature democracy and there was a recognition from the start that many of the options available to the United States could prove counter-productive.

Even so, events subsequent to the 1984 election appear to demonstrate a considerable determination to bring about a more acceptable policy from New Zealand, and the roots of this determination stem from developments in US foreign and defence policy in the 1970s and early 1980s.

The Faltering Globalism

The 'rise to globalism' of the United States in the 1940s was a direct result of its experience in the Second World War and had political, economic and military causes.[1] With the waning power of Great Britain and the temporary neutralisation of the economic power of Germany and Japan, the United States became the focus of western power in the Cold War. Its economic base had been hugely expanded in the war effort, with impressive developments in electronics, chemicals and engineering, and the widespread application of new techniques of mass production.

Militarily, the United States had fought major wars on two fronts, with the Pacific War leading to the development of a navy with global power projection capabilities. While much of this was run down in the early post-war years, the experience in Korea and, later, in Vietnam, ensured that the United States developed into the only nation with a truly global military reach. This was heightened by the dismantling of the European colonial empires but was concentrated initially in the Pacific, South East Asia and Western Europe. Eventually, by the end of the 1960s, the United States was even replacing Britain and France in the Middle East.

Against this background, there were three serious setbacks for the United States in the early 1970s. One was internal, the developing Watergate scandal, which led to Nixon's resignation and the weak presidency of Gerald Ford. Even with the influence of Henry Kissinger at hand, US foreign policy was somewhat stifled in the early 1970s.

Two further problems, the aftermath of Vietnam and the 1973–4 oil crisis, were more directly within the foreign policy arena. The slow and painful withdrawal from Vietnam was recognised as a defeat; the United States had been beaten by a militarily weaker yet determined adversary – the F–4 Phantom had been beaten by the guerilla on a bicycle.

The defeat in Vietnam brought into question the ability of the United States to act in what it perceived to be its rightful world policing role, leading to a difficult debate within a country still split by the bitter domestic divisions over the Vietnam War. One effect, during the early 1970s, was a certain reluctance to become involved in further exercises in the projection of military force, but this coincided almost exactly with a new crisis which some believed required just such action.

---

1. See Stephen E. Ambrose, *Rise to Globalism: American Foreign Policy, 1938–80*, Penguin Books, London and New York, 1980.

Towards the end of the 1973 Arab–Israeli War, a group of Arab oil-producing states sought to use their influence over oil markets for political purposes. With Israel posed to snatch a major military victory from what had initially been a potential disaster, the Arab members of OPEC attempted to use their 'producer power' to bring pressure on Israel, particularly through its prime supporter, the United States. They recognised that Israeli military success in the conflict was dependent on the rapid replacement of war-time losses by air-lift from the United States and on 17 October 1973 instigated a three-point plan to apply pressure. This comprised a 15 per cent cut-back in oil production to engineer a modest scarcity, an increase in crude oil prices averaging 72 per cent and an embargo on oil exports to Israel's two strongest supporters, the United States and the Netherlands.

The immediate impact on the United States was small, as it was not yet a major oil importer, but action by the whole membership of OPEC in the following three months included a further doubling of the price of crude oil. By May 1974 the price of oil was up by around 400 per cent on prices before the crisis, with a pronounced psychological, not to say economic, impact on western industrialised countries. Their access to a key resource was being challenged from a wholly unexpected Third World source. This was without parallel in the post-colonial era and gave rise to an uncomfortable feeling of impotence.

Worse still, the western industrialised countries were not able to act in unison, not least because the transnational oil companies were benefiting greatly from the price increases and would not act together with governments to exert pressure on OPEC. If the United States had not experienced the reversals of Vietnam, it might have been more willing to intervene militarily in the Middle East, but it was not clear that it even had the military capability to do so, and prospects for joint western action were minimal.[2] By the middle 1970s Pax Americana seemed, at best, limited, if not tarnished.

The Carter Approach

Carter was elected in 1976 against the background of a country unsure of itself or its world role, and increasingly careful about becoming ensnared

2. Congressional Research Service, Library of Congress, *Oil Fields as Military Objectives: A Feasibility Study*, US Government and Printing Office, Washington, 1975.

in new foreign involvements, and at a time of world inflation and economic uncertainty. He appeared at first to be an out-of-town liberal populist, with a foreign policy involving greater concern for human rights than that of any post-war US administration.[3] This concentration on human rights was seen by many traditional liberal democrats as the only way to allow American liberal values to have their head. Moreover, in countering more conservative opinions, such an emphasis had the advantage that a US foreign policy stressing human rights would be seen to create continuing difficulties for the Soviet Union and its associated repressive regimes in Eastern Europe and elsewhere.

An initially less significant aspect of the early Carter years was his relatively strong commitment to nuclear arms control and disarmament, stemming not least from direct personal experience of the realities of nuclear technology earlier in his career. It is worth noting, however, that he did not have the same attitude towards conventional military forces. Here, a modest process of re-equipment and selective expansion included the establishment of the Joint Rapid Deployment Task Force (JRDTF), known popularly as the rapid deployment force. This was established by 1979 as an intended integrated military force of over a quarter of a million troops backed by amphibious forces, carrier battle groups and land-based air power which was designed for intervention principally in the Middle East but potentially anywhere else in the world.

Contrary to general belief, US military spending had declined (in real terms) under Nixon and Ford, after peaking in 1968 under Johnson at the height of the Vietnam War. For the first three years of the Carter administration, this decline was halted, with a significant expansion in 1980. Nevertheless, Carter pursued an active nuclear arms control policy, culminating in the signing of the SALT II strategic arms agreement with Brezhnev in Vienna in 1979.

Carter's generally liberal stance on foreign policy, especially towards the Third World, was an orientation which was bitterly opposed by right-wing analysts and policy specialists, by no means restricted to the Republican Party, and there were increasing tensions within the Carter administration, centred particularly on the views of Carter's National Security Adviser, Zbigniew Brzezinski. The 'hawks' saw Carter as maintaining a weak foreign policy which, by its emphasis on human rights, undermined the firm, stable right-wing governments which were so essen-

---

3. See Lloyd C. Gardner, *A Covenant With Power: America and World Order from Wilson to Reagan*, Macmillan, London, 1984.

tial in the battle against communist expansionism.

Furthermore, while Carter talked to the Soviets and sought a SALT II agreement, Soviet nuclear capabilities continued to grow. Throughout the late 1970s, right-wing analysts worried about two aspects of Soviet military power. One was the development of several new types of nuclear missile. The Soviet Intercontinental Ballistic Missile (ICBM) force was being modernised with SS–17, SS–18 and SS–19 missiles, all with multiple independently-targetable re-entry vehicles (MIRVs), and, at least in the case of the SS–18, carrying warheads with a destructive force and accuracy sufficient to threaten US ICBM siloes. A related concern was the deployment from 1977 of the mobile three-warhead MIRVed SS–20 intermediate-range ballistic missile, able to target the whole of Europe and Eastern Asia from bases throughout the Soviet Union.

The second aspect of Soviet power was the continuing development of the Soviet Navy from an essentially coastal force into a modern integrated navy with the capacity to project power throughout the world. The first *Kiev*-class aircraft-carrier was commissioned in 1975, and a second in 1978. That same year, the first *Kirov*-class battle-cruiser commenced fitting out near Leningrad and the first *Slava*-class cruiser was launched the following year. In some ways more significant was the deployment of a large amphibious warfare ship, the *Ivan Rogov*, with a displacement of 13,000 tons full load, more than three times the size of previous Soviet amphibious warships. The *Ivan Rogov* had a range of at least 4,000 miles and could carry a naval infantry battalion of over 500 men with up to 20 tanks. None of these developments was sufficient to counter-balance the impressive power projection capabilities of the US Navy, but they represented a sea-change in Soviet maritime capabilities at a time when US developments seemed, by contrast, to be limited.

Soviet power projection, and in particular the possibility of the Soviet Union being able to project forces into the Pacific (previously regarded almost as a US 'lake'), was coupled with fears about the potential of the new Soviet ICBMs thus producing a mood of frustration with the Carter administration's defence policies. In particular, a belief that US nuclear forces were becoming susceptible to Soviet missiles, the so-called 'window of vulnerability', became a major political issue during the latter years of the Carter administration, exacerbated by reports from a variety of generally Republican-orientated right-wing policy groups.

Carter had cancelled one major defence programme, the B–1 strategic bomber, back in 1977, but the changing climate was partly responsible for an administration re-assessment which resulted eventually in the decision to promote the air-launched cruise missile as a force multiplier for the older B–52 bomber. In Europe proposals sought to expand NATO's theatre nuclear forces with a deployment of 464 ground-launched cruise missiles and 108 Pershing 2 ballistic missiles, ostensibly balancing out the Soviet SS–20. Even by the end of 1979 the developments in Europe were a cause of growing public concern, leading eventually to a powerfully re-awakened anti-nuclear movement in the early 1980s.

Although the Carter administration had embarked on a process of selective re-armament by its last year in office, its perceived foreign policy orientation was still broadly liberal. As a result, the Reagan presidential campaign was able to derive powerful political capital from two major foreign policy dilemmas which were facing Carter by early 1980.

The first was the Soviet intervention in Afghanistan from December 1979, a military build-up which could easily be represented by Republicans as nothing short of a full-scale invasion. Combined with the problems in Poland resulting from developing trade union activism, this appeared to show the Soviet Union in a new mood – determined to control dissent with rigour within its sphere of influence. The Afghanistan intervention could even be seen as part of a more insidious Soviet grand plan to increase its influence throughout South West Asia extending eventually to direct access to the Arabian Sea and Indian Ocean.

An even greater problem was the rapidly deteriorating situation in Iran. The downfall of the Shah in January 1979 had removed a key ally of the United States in the Middle East, a state seen as the lynch-pin of US efforts to contain Soviet influence in the region. The seeming inability of the United States to foresee this development, or influence subsequent affairs, was damaging enough, but the taking of more than 50 US diplomats as hostages on 4 November 1979 was little short of catastrophic.

The Iranian hostage crisis was to dominate US domestic politics for much of 1980, the more so after a rescue attempt in April ended in failure. The Reagan campaign was able to represent Iran as the final failure of Carter's foreign policy, with an impotent US government trying to deal with a rigorously anti-American regime. The re-arming of America became a key-note of the campaign and the 'ghost of Vietnam' could finally be laid to rest in this determination to make America strong again.

The Early Reagan Years

As we have seen, the re-arming process was underway before Reagan took office, with the Fiscal Year 1981 defence budget (October 1980 to September 1981) set to be the highest for ten years. Even so, the early actions of the Reagan administration in this area were directed to a much greater expansion, its rhetoric on the Soviet 'evil empire' being matched by its determination to restore the United States to its global pre-eminence.

In the early 1980s, two quite separate areas of concentration were to become significant: the expansion of nuclear forces and the enhancement of US military force projection capabilities, especially through the US Navy. Each is of considerable significance in the context of the New Zealand experience of the middle 1980s and is worth detailed examination. The administration's response to the apparent neglect of nuclear forces under Carter was to increase substantially the budgets for strategic and intermediate-range nuclear weapons and, in addition, to accelerate research into advanced weapons systems. At the strategic level, the B–1 strategic bomber was rescued from the scrap-yard, and a major development programme resulted, by July 1985, in the deployment of the first of a highly modified version, the B–1B. One hundred were built over a three-year period. The M–X ICBM, named 'Peacekeeper' by Reagan, completed its development and was deployed from late 1986. Work progressed on a new small mobile 'Midgetman' ICBM, large numbers of the Trident C4 submarine-launched missile were deployed and work on the much more advanced Trident D5 successor was accelerated.[4]

The heavy investment in research and development in the early 1980s concentrated on improving missile accuracy, developing earth-penetrating warheads and investigating the feasibility of third-generation directional nuclear weapons. Some of these programmes received an additional boost with the funding of the Strategic Defense Initiative (SDI) programme in the mid-1980s.

At the intermediate level, the administration proceeded with plans for the comprehensive deployment of nuclear and conventional cruise missiles on US Navy submarines and surface warships regarded as essential for extended deterrence. Around 4,000 were to be deployed in the mid- and late 1980s, with 750 of them nuclear-armed. There were to be 198 submarines and surface ships equipped with these new missiles, but

4. Paul Rogers, *Guide to Nuclear Weapons*, Berg Publishers, Oxford and New York, 1988, pp. 5–21.

there was no intention of indicating which would be nuclear-tipped. The sea-launched cruise missile programme was seen as a key aspect of the rebuilding of US naval strength, and the dual-capable nature of the weapons made the navy's 'neither confirm nor deny' policy even more significant.

While the navy's cruise missile programme had obvious implications for countries such as New Zealand, it was the deployment of ground-launched cruise missiles (GLCMs) and the Pershing 2 missile in Western Europe which had the more immediate impact. In all five countries concerned – Belgium, Holland, Italy, West Germany and Britain – public opposition developed rapidly in the early 1980s. Mass demonstrations were the visible result, but a more significant development was the mounting opposition within major political parties on the left. In Britain, the Labour Party adopted a non-nuclear approach, applying this to Britain's own nuclear weapons and those of the United States based in the country. In West Germany, the SPD adopted an increasingly anti-nuclear stance, pressed hard by the more radical Green Party, and in most other European members of NATO, political opposition to cruise and Pershing 2 was substantial.

The key period for the United States was 1983–4. Anti-nuclear sentiments in Western Europe were at their peak, and even in the United States, the substantial freeze movement was attracting much attention. NATO tried to defuse the issue by announcing major unilateral cuts in shorter-range tactical nuclear weapons at the end of 1983, but the 1,400 warheads to be removed were mainly obsolete and due for withdrawal in any case, and the impact on public opinion was limited.

By early 1984, and in the run-up to the New Zealand general election, some analysts were suggesting that the European anti-nuclear campaigns were past their peak. The initial deployment of the new missiles from December 1983 onwards was thought likely to bring a grudging accept-ance of the new circumstances, but it was clear that the anti-nuclear movements would retain considerable strength for some time to come.

In this context, New Zealand did present a problem. It was a relatively isolated country of minimal strategic significance, but it did have close cultural and historic links with Britain. Far more important, however, was that here was an anti-nuclear *government* coming to power. Oppositional peace movements can be significant determinants of public opinion, but a political party taking power on an anti-nuclear ticket was a far more serious matter, and could have a significant psychological impact on parties in Western Europe. In the context of heightened global concern over the nuclear arms race, clearly New Zealand was likely to be a problem for the United States.

The US Navy and Force Projection

The re-arming of America so central to the Reagan administration's foreign policy orientation was, in the dominant perception of western public opinion, primarily concerned with a much greater commitment to nuclear weapons. In reality, this was just one of two parallel trends. The second was concerned with re-building the capacity of the United States to project military force anywhere in the world, a capacity which had been a major casualty in the aftermath of the Vietnam War.

While New Zealand may appear peripheral in terms of the strategic interests of the United States, when one takes into account the considerable emphasis on naval strategy and force projection in the early 1980s, a rather different picture emerges, especially as New Zealand's nuclear-free policy was, as far as the United States was concerned, focused on a ban on port visits from US warships.

In the run-up to the 1980 US Presidential elections, a major issue had become the perceived run-down of the US Navy, and an important campaigning point centred on the demand from the Reagan team for a 600-ship navy. When the administration took office, the Navy Secretary was John Lehman, a highly articulate and effective publicist for the navy who was to remain in office for the next six years. Under Lehman, the navy was to seek major budget increases, especially for new ships, and also refined and eventually published what became known as the Maritime Strategy, a detailed policy statement for the navy and marine corps. As Norman Friedman remarks in a recent study, this is novel for two reasons:

> First, the focus on war-fighting strategy is unusual for the period since about 1950; note that the word 'strategic' is almost universally applied to the application of long-range nuclear weapons, not to an overall concept of warfare. Second, it is unusual in American history for the national or military strategy or even one of its components to be made so explicit.[5]

5. Norman Friedman, *The US Maritime Strategy*, Jane's, London and New York, 1988.

The Maritime Strategy was developed in the early 1980s, first receiving detailed open discussion in a supplement to the Proceedings of the US Naval Institute in January 1986 which included papers by Lehman and Admiral James D. Watkins.[6] The Maritime Strategy is concerned with controlling the 'violent peace' of the late 1980s and combines the ability to wage direct war on the Soviet Union, should that come to pass, with the ability to confront and resolve a variety of Third World crises and confrontations.[7]

In the ultimate eventuality of war with the Soviet Union, it is assumed that if deterrence breaks down there will be three broad stages of confrontation short of full-scale nuclear exchange: *transition to war*, which comprises mobilisation and forward deployment of forces; *seizing the initiative*, which involves initial attacks on Soviet strategic ballistic missile submarines, 'bottling up' of Soviet naval forces and preservation of lines of communication'; and *carrying the war to the enemy*, or favourable war execution and termination.

This implies a generally offensive stance requiring global power projection capabilities, an aspect which is clear from the following description of the final phase of conflict:

> The tasks in this phase are similar to those in earlier phases, but must be more aggressively applied as we seek war termination on terms favourable to the United States and its allies. Our goal would be to complete the destruction of all the Soviet fleets begun in Phase II. This destruction allows us to threaten the bases and support structure of the Soviet navy in all theatres with both air and amphibious power. Such threats are quite credible to the Soviets. At the same time, anti-submarine warfare forces would continue to destroy Soviet submarines, including ballistic missile submarines, thus reducing the attractiveness of nuclear escalation by changing the nuclear balance in our favour.
>
> During the final phase, the United States and its allies would press home the initiative world-wide, while continuing to support air and land campaigns, maintaining sealift, and keeping sea lines of communication open. Amphibious forces, up to the size of a full Marine Amphibious Force, would be used to regain territory. In addition, the full weight of the carrier battle forces could continue to 'roll up' the Soviets on the flanks, contribute to the battle on the Central Front, or carry the

6. 'The Maritime Strategy', supplement to the *Proceedings of the U.S. Naval Institute*, January 1988, p. 8.
7. Paul Rogers, 'Force Projection and Third World Militarization', *Working Paper for the Conference on Militarisation of the Third World*, Canadian Institute for International Peace and Security, Ottawa, January 1987.

war to the Soviets. These tough operations, close to the Soviet mother-land, could even come earlier than the last phase.[8]

A picture thus emerges of global military operations against the Soviet Union and its peripheral assets, involving the allies of the United States in an overtly aggressive series of military operations aimed at pre-empting Soviet actions.

Much of the recent enhancement of US naval capabilities has been in the light of this approach, but it remains just one part of the Maritime Strategy, for the naval forces can just as well be applied to lesser Third World conflicts including what may be described as proxy conflicts with perceived Soviet surrogates. Indeed, surface combatants, especially carrier battle groups and amphibious forces, are crucial to a strategy for controlling the violent peace in the Third World when this threatens US interests.

A violent peace strategy differs from the kind of global war strategy with the Soviet Union in three broad respects. Firstly, a wartime strategy concentrates on countering overt Soviet aggression while 'peacetime strategy objectives are more diffuse and perhaps best characterized as furthering an ill-defined set of interests of which countering the Soviets is only part, although a very important part.'[9]

Secondly, a violent peace strategy is inherently less structured and clear-cut in its objectives and processes. Finally, political and diplomatic considerations may dominate or circumscribe military considerations, at least in the early stages of a particular crisis. Within this context the major aims of a violent peace strategy are: protecting sea lines of communication and transit rights; allowing the United States continued access to resources and markets; and demonstrating US interests overseas.

Such a violent peace strategy depends on adequate force projection capability, and there have been six broad areas of enhancement during the 1980s.[10]

(1) The number of carrier battle groups is rising from thirteen to fifteen with several in reserve. No other country has comparable sea-based aviation power; just three US carrier battle groups deploy more

8. Admiral James D. Watkins, 'The Maritime Strategy', p. 11.
9. R. Robinson Harris and Joseph Benkert, 'Is That All There Is?', *Proceedings of the U.S. Naval Institute*, October 1985.
10. See Rogers, 'Force Projection', pp. 16–24.

fixed-wing aircraft than all the carrier-borne forces of the remaining countries of the world.

(2) Four battleships have been upgraded and returned to service, equipped with their original 16″ calibre main armament as well as Tomahawk and Harpoon cruise missile launchers. The main armament enables each ship to fire nine one-ton high explosive shells or sub-munitions packages over a fifteen mile range simultaneously. No other nation possesses anything remotely on the scale of this naval bombardment potential.

(3) The Marine Corps is currently the world's most powerful amphibious force, its 198,000 personnel being more than ten times that of the Soviet Union. It maintains over forty large amphibious warfare ships, integral air support and a wide range of specialised equipment including tactical nuclear weapons. Qualitative improvements in the 1980s include deployment of over 300 advanced AV–8B jump jets, the new *Wasp*-class amphibious assault ship and the introduction of armed air-cushion vehicles for coastal assault.

(4) Logistic support for force projection has been upgraded with eight large fast container-ships being converted into Fast Sealift Support ships, capable of transporting most of the equipment for a complete armoured division. A Near Term Prepositioning Force of up to seventeen ships, based at Diego Garcia in the Indian Ocean, provides broadly similar support for a Marine Amphibious Brigade of 12,000 troops and supporting personnel, being able to maintain them in combat without other re-supply for thirty days. This is being replaced in due course by thirteen much larger Maritime Prepositioning ships capable of supporting a 50,000 strong Marine Amphibious Force for thirty days.

(5) In 1985, the rapid deployment force was elevated to the status of a unified military command, Central Command or CENTCOM, with responsibilities for nineteen countries of South West Asia and North East Africa stretching in an arc from Pakistan to Kenya. Forces assigned to CENTCOM now number over 300,000, including an army brigade of over 4,000 troops at twenty hours readiness. The logistical pre-positioning already described is integral to the operations of this command.

(6) One of the areas of most rapid expansion has been that of special forces. A Unified Command for Special Forces was established in the United States covering units such as the Green Berets, Navy

SEAL (Sea-Air-Land) forces, Air Force Special Operations Squadrons, Rangers and Delta Force. All these groups are concerned in particular with low intensity operations, and most of their experience in recent years has been in the Third World. The expansion of Special Operations Forces in the early Reagan years can be judged by the increase in active duty manpower by 30 per cent from 1981 to 1985, giving a total of 14,900. Planned figures for 1990 are 20,900.

This combination of a more globally assertive Maritime Strategy with a comprehensive enhancement of the navy and marine corps resources was well under way by 1984. It had greatly boosted morale in the navy and had given rise to a confidence that the United States had finally overcome the legacy of the Vietnam War. For a long-time ally such as New Zealand to decide, at such a time, to take action which directly affected the activities of the US Navy was viewed with undisguised annoyance.

Even so, one might counter this by remembering the relatively isolated position of New Zealand in geo-strategic terms. While certainly an occasion for frustration and concern, New Zealand appeared superficially peripheral to US foreign policy and strategic interests. In reality, just as cultural links made New Zealand's action a cause of concern in the context of European anti-nuclear sentiments, so its South West Pacific location and, in particular, the impact of its actions on other Pacific nations, was also a source of concern.

In part, this was due to a fear of Soviet expansion of power projection into the Pacific, consequent on the steady build-up of the Soviet Pacific fleet operating out of bases on the Soviet Pacific sea-board. At the height of the New Zealand ships-ban controversy, in April 1985, the Soviet Union deployed a full-scale carrier battle group, based on the VTOL (vertical take-off and landing) carrier *Novorossiisk*, out into the Western Pacific. The nine-ship task force sailed over 6,000 miles and is believed to have been the first carrier battle group modelled on US Navy lines ever assembled by the Soviet Navy.[11] While this came some months after the 1984 New Zealand general election, it was a result of a Pacific naval build-up which had been under way for several years and had included the establishment of a substantial naval base at Cam Ranh Bay in Vietnam, ironically using many facilities constructed by the United States during the Vietnam War.

11. Ibid.

The increasing importance of the West Pacific economies and Pacific trade routes to the United States, itself a characteristic of increasing US reliance on resources from overseas, gave even greater cause for concern over New Zealand's policy. Much of the concern with enhancing force projection capabilities was rooted in US requirements for stable resource supplies and, as we saw earlier, two key peace-time functions of the Maritime Strategy were protecting sea lines of communication and allowing continued US access to resources and markets.

While concerns over resources access had originally been focused on Middle East oil supplies, with the rapid deployment force being a direct response to the events of 1973–4, by the early 1980s resource access was of much wider interest, especially to the military. In part, this was due to a continuing decline of the mineral resource base of the United States itself and hence the increasing need to import from overseas. It was also due to the particular demands of the re-armament programme, especially for strategic raw materials crucial to arms production, such as metals used in specialised ferro-alloys.

These concerns dominated much of the thinking of the Department of Defense analysts in the early 1980s, and were well expressed in the policy section of the US Joint Chiefs of Staff Military Posture for Fiscal Year 1982, published in 1981:

> The dependency of the United States on foreign sources of non-fuels, minerals and metals has increased sharply over the last two decades. Taking a list of the top 25 such imported commodities, in 1960 our dependency averaged 54 per cent. In 1980, our dependency for the same items averages 70 per cent. In fact our dependency is 75 per cent or more on foreign countries where war could, in the foreseeable future, deny us our supplies of bauxite, chromite, cobalt, columbium, manganese, nickel and tantalum. These metals and minerals figure in the manufacture of aircraft, motor vehicles, appliances, high strength or stainless steels, magnets, jet engine parts, cryogenic devices, gyroscopes, superconductors, capacitors, vacuum tubes, electro-optics, printed circuits, contacts, connectors, armor plate and instrumentation, among other things.[12]

After giving a detailed account of increasing US dependence on Middle East oil supplies, the Posture Statement went on to stress the Soviet

---

12. US Joint Chiefs of Staff, *Military Posture Statement, Fiscal Year 1982*, US Government Printing Office, Washington, 1981, p. 3.

position of near self-sufficiency of resource supplies in comparison with US vulnerability. It elaborated on this aspect by making the connection between that vulnerability and Soviet expansionism:

> The Soviet Union's self-sufficiency in fossil fuels – oil, natural gas and coal – is mirrored by virtual self-sufficiency in other minerals. The Soviet Union must import only six minerals critical to its defense industry, and only two of these are brought in for as much as 50 per cent of requirements. In contrast, the United States relies on foreign sources to supply amounts in excess of 50 per cent of its needs for some 32 minerals essential for our military and industrial base.[13]

While several key metals came primarily from Southern and Central Africa, including platinum and cobalt, the West Pacific resource base was growing in importance. This now included chromite from the Philippines, bauxite and manganese from Australia, columbium and tantalum from Malaysia, Thailand and Australia, and nickel from Australia and the Philippines. More widely used resources included tin from Malaysia and natural rubber from Malaysia, Thailand and Indonesia.

In all these cases, major shipping routes crossed the Pacific and both the sources of supply and the shipment routes were seen as vulnerable to Soviet action. As the Posture Statement concluded in relation to problems of resource access:

> The foregoing dangers should not be regarded as wholly a matter of markets or access threatened by regional political considerations or events, for the fact is that the US is engaged in competition against the Soviet Union. Whether or not we choose to regard our relationship in competitive terms, the Russians assuredly do.
>
> To cope with the dangers of the 1980s and meet the Soviet challenge, the US must continue to pursue a strategy that draws upon the combined resources of allied and friendly nations to full and mutual advantage.[14]

In summary, an aggressive global naval strategy had been developed by 1984 with one of its key concerns the need to ensure US access to its overseas resource supplies. The Pacific was becoming increasingly significant at a time when the Soviet Union was, for the first time, beginning to

13. Ibid.
14. Ibid.

demonstrate its own power projection capabilities. Yet just at this time, a previously trusted, if not 'taken-for-granted', ally, with some influence in the Pacific, chose to implement a policy which had a direct effect on the US Navy.

Conclusions

This chapter has sought to place the 1984 New Zealand general election and the victory of the Lange administration in the context of US foreign and security policy, emphasising two aspects of particular significance. After the post-Vietnam traumas and the troubles of the Carter administration, the United States under Reagan sought vigorously to re-assert US power and influence. In the military sphere two important aspects of this new outlook were directly relevant to the New Zealand case.

The nuclear re-arming had resulted in public opposition at home, but very much more widespread concern in Western Europe. All the major governments remained supportive of the new developments, but opposition parties were strong and New Zealand, while geographically distant, had close cultural links with the UK. Moreover, it had a new government which had, uniquely, taken a firm anti-nuclear stance. Such a change might well be contagious.

New Zealand's policy was of more exact concern because it had influence in an area of the world which was of increasing importance to the United States and was regarded as very much its own area of interest; a rather large back-yard certainly, but still a back-yard. Moreover, the implementation of the New Zealand policy was directly related to the prime exponent of US military strategy in the Pacific, the US Navy.

All this was in the context of a United States foreign policy which was, in spite of some tensions, still being backed by its major allies, such as Britain and West Germany. To an extent, the support of allied governments was taken for granted, certainly in the Department of Defense if not entirely in the more circumspect State Department. In all three senses, nuclear strategy, maritime strategy and allied support, the election of the Lange government was an unwelcome event.

Its nuclear-free policies clearly needed to be countered, and a major world power such as the United States had a range of options available to it. By no means all were appropriate, and many might prove counter-productive. Before examining the actual sequence of events and the choices

46

made by the United States, it is therefore appropriate to review the methods available to bring the New Zealand government round to a more 'acceptable' stance.

CHAPTER 4

Responding to Labour: US Foreign Policy Options Towards New Zealand

Facing continuing opposition to its nuclear weapons deployments in Western Europe and the Pacific, the United States government now had the added problem of a newly elected government in New Zealand which appeared likely to implement a ban on port visits from nuclear-armed or nuclear-powered warships. Moreover, the latter government had come to power following an intense public debate on the nuclear issue and with polls showing considerable support for a nuclear ships ban. A mandate clearly existed. In other respects, however, the policies of the new government were broadly centrist, if not right-wing on economic and fiscal matters. It was not therefore a government which could easily be represented as dangerously left-wing in all its aspects.

US foreign policy was therefore directed quite specifically towards the government's policy on nuclear issues and had three broad aims. The first and immediate task was to moderate the policy on nuclear ship visits, thus avoiding the United States having either to change its 'neither-confirm-nor-deny policy' or abandon port visits to the country.

A longer-term aim would be to persuade the New Zealand government of the need to maintain a commitment to nuclear deterrence, especially extended deterrence, as an essential underpinning of US and allied security. This would enable the existing security relationship to be maintained and avoid New Zealand becoming an example to public opinion in allied countries, especially in Western Europe and the Pacific.

Finally, it would be desirable to influence public opinion in New Zealand away from its majority anti-nuclear sentiments. This would ensure that any changes in governmental attitude would have a firm foundation in public opinion and electoral behaviour. It would ultimately help to ensure that the nuclear issue would not be a significant feature of future New Zealand electoral politics.

The methods available to the United States to execute these foreign policy objectives were, in theory, wide-ranging. They covered the full range of instruments of foreign policy, including military, economic, diplomatic and propaganda methods and pressures. In practice, its scope for manoeuvre was much more limited by the nature of its cultural and political links with New Zealand and the risk of particular actions being counter-productive.

Even so, it is useful to review the broad range of options available, in order to put into context the actions actually employed by the United States and its allies after the 1984 election.

Military Options

The most extreme instrument of foreign policy is the use of military force extending ultimately to a declaration of war. In practice, in recent decades, formal declarations of war have been rare, but use of military force has been common. Most of the hundred or more conflicts since 1945 have been occasioned by the process of retreat from empire, but super-power rivalries have been significant factors. In addition, Third World conflicts have arisen through disputes over boundaries, resources and questions of regional influence.

There have been many examples of superpower intervention, most commonly by the United States, where these have involved direct use of military force. US intervention itself has ranged from 'use of force', as in the intervention in Grenada, to 'show of force', as in a number of naval deployments in the Middle East and Central America. The Reagan administration had engaged in such activities prior to the 1984 New Zealand election, although the largest use of force would occur three years later with the build-up of US military power in the Persian Gulf in 1987.

In addition to direct military intervention and 'show of force' activities, a wide range of subversive interventions is available. These range from bribery and dissemination of covert propaganda through to support for guerilla organisations, unofficial intervention by special forces, use of surrogates and even political assassinations.

All have been used by many countries in the post-war world, and most were employed in various arenas by the Reagan administration in the early 1980s. Even so, there is no evidence that the US considered intervention or direct subversion in the New Zealand case. The problem, rather, was that the United States considered that various forms of intervention elsewhere were legitimate instruments of foreign policy and New Zealand's very specific action on the nuclear ships issue could easily be seen as part of a more general opposition to US foreign policy in its new, more confident and assertive phase.

By the mid-1980s, the US administration saw itself very much in the business of 'keeping the violent peace'. Nicaragua, Lebanon and Grenada were considered to be examples of this, and they would be followed by Libya and the Gulf. Yet here was a previously trusted ally apparently prepared to question the United States in its newly assured position.

Major sectors of opinion in the United States regarded the policies of the new government as falling grievously short of the behaviour required of a close ally, but even the most antagonistic sources of opinion recognised the impossibility of enforcing a change of policy by any kind of direct intervention.

Diplomatic Influence

In seeking to pursue its policy of effecting change in New Zealand's attitudes, the United States was thus effectively restricted to a wide range of potential actions stopping short of intervention. The routine methods relate to diplomatic and information/propaganda actions. The more forceful methods include economic and political pressures.

K. J. Holsti defines the functions of diplomats as protection of nationals, symbolic representation, obtaining information and providing advice and policy formulation.[1] In the New Zealand example, the extent and depth of anti-nuclear sentiments in New Zealand and the result of the 1984 election appears to have caused some surprise to the United States, implying that either the US diplomatic mission in New Zealand had under-estimated

---

1. K. J. Holsti, *International Politics* (3rd edn), Prentice-Hall, London, 1983, p. 168.

developments, or Washington had failed to take seriously the advice being offered.

Once the election had taken place, the work of the Wellington Embassy increased in importance. It acted as a channel for Washington's views to be communicated to the New Zealand government through the usual diplomatic means and, more importantly, it acted as an informal two-way conduit for exchanging views.

Diplomats function routinely through formal exchanges governed by protocol, and political displeasure can be indicated by many means, including expulsions or downgrading of representational status. Where it is thought necessary to influence political attitudes, any decrease in diplomatic status or numbers of personnel may be counter-productive, especially in limiting the informal work of a diplomatic mission. Such work includes maintenance of a wide range of social contacts among opinion formers of the host country. In circumstances of controversy it is possible to use these contacts to assess the status of the position taken by the host country's government, analyse the extent of opposition and, in an active way, indicate one's position and the possible effects of the controversy on mutual relations. It is hardly surprising that after the 1984 election, the US extended its diplomatic mission in New Zealand by opening an office in Christchurch, the largest centre of population on the South Island.

Routine monitoring of the host country's media, especially editorial comment, will be accompanied by extensive probing of views of government and opposition members of the legislature, newspaper editors, business, financial and academic opinion formers, the military and, where possible, relevant activist groups. Annual party conferences and conventions are attended, not just for the formal agenda but for fringe meetings and informal contact. Private opinion polls may be taken which may probe not just the popularity of particular policies but the likely public reaction to foreign responses to those policies. Democracies have the advantage that lawful oppositions are available to be aided and influenced but they have the disadvantage that firm reaction to national policies can easily be represented as foreign interference and can thereby prove counter-productive.

Formal and informal diplomatic channels thus allow a diplomatic mission to assess the policies of a host country and analyse the extent of their support. These are communicated to the foreign affairs ministry or department with possible recommendations for action. The role of a diplomatic mission in actively formulating foreign policy has diminished greatly with improvements in communications, but 'on-site' assessments are still of considerable value.

Similarly, the action of communicating the attitude of one's government to the host government can strictly be done without the use of a diplomatic mission. In practice, however, a mission has such a wide range of channels of communication, both formal and informal, that reactions can readily be gauged with greater accuracy, and damaging counter-reactions mitigated if not avoided. If a particular policy has been determined, a diplomatic mission can communicate it directly to the host country's foreign affairs ministry and thence to the whole government. In extreme cases, and if the diplomatic mission has sufficient status, an interview can be sought with the head of state or government. More commonly, however, informal channels will be used, both to government, by means of social occasions, or to opinion formers, such as editors, civil servants and others.

It may be appropriate for a formal public occasion to be used. In the run-up to the 1987 UK general election, the then US Secretary of Defense, Caspar Weinberger, was due to give a lecture to the English-Speaking Union in London, and used the occasion to communicate his views, in a suitably veiled yet unmistakeable manner, on the inadvisability of a British government altering its defence policy. The lecture, though to an apparently non-party political body, was widely reported by the media in the context of the imminent general election in which Labour's non-nuclear defence policy was a major issue.

Similarly, the US Ambassador to London at the time, Charles Price III, was apt to give lectures on the theme of European security, which would be released to the UK press. Interestingly, such lectures tended to be given when he was on home visits to the United States, though they would be released to the British press from the London Embassy. The protocol of not interfering in the internal affairs of the host country was thus maintained but the views could still be communicated.

In summary, normal diplomatic relations allow a wide range of means of exercising powers of persuasion. They range from informal and indeed confidential discussions through to formal indications of policy positions communicated through correct channels.

Information, Propaganda and the Influencing of Opinion

While the policy functions of diplomatic missions are essentially two-way – assessing the political environment and communicating positions – they merge almost imperceptibly into the more dynamic role of influencing opinion. All diplomatic missions are concerned with providing information, whether it be commercial, educational or even related to tourism. Where mere provision of information merges into propaganda is not always easy to determine, but T.H. Qualter's definition of propaganda is useful: 'the deliberate attempt by some individual or group to form, control, or alter the attitudes of other groups by the use of instruments of communication, with the intention that in any given situation the reaction of those so influenced will be that desired by the propagandist.'[2] As K.J. Holsti comments, propaganda is not necessarily concerned with promulgating untruths, but it does have four key features: the intention of changing attitudes, opinions or behaviour; the symbols used by the communicator; the media of communication; and the audience or 'target' for the propaganda.[3] While not merely the promulgation of falsehoods, propaganda is rarely concerned with the whole truth, rather with selective dissemination of facts and opinions supporting the desired change of opinion.

While diplomatic missions will be engaged, to an extent, in propaganda, the means of conducting a campaign extend far beyond such facilities. Radio and, more recently, television stations are commonly employed, and most larger governments have extensive information dissemination organisations which are concerned primarily with promoting government policy overseas. They are often responsible for the radio and TV services aimed at overseas audiences, and normally include news agencies and film and video services. When there is a degree of urgency involved, as in the need to counter the policy of a newly elected government of an ally, existing 'information' services can be expanded to cope with the extra needs.

The largest western government information organisation is the United States Information Agency (USIA),[4] established in 1954 and having among its functions:

2. T. H. Qualter, *Propaganda and Psychological Warfare*, Random House, New York, 1962, p. 27.
3. Holsti, *International Politics*, p. 195.
4. It should be noted that the USIA is sometimes also referred to as the United States Information *Service* (USIS). For the sake of consistency it will be referred to as the USIA in this book.

(1) To explain and interpret to people overseas the meaning and purposes of American foreign policies.

(2) To serve as a source of accurate non-sensational news abroad without competing with private American news sources.

(3) To present the full sweep of American life and culture to the people of the world in order to correct misconceptions and to combat false or distorted pictures of the United States.[5]

Government information agencies operate both in public and in private. While the agency may produce its own material, it will also rely on other government departments. In its efforts to communicate its views on the nature of the Soviet military threat to western security in the early 1980s, the US Department of Defense commenced publishing an annual report, *Soviet Military Power*, in 1981, which contained considerable detail on the Soviet armed forces and Soviet strategy. This became a regular feature of the defence media scene in the mid-1980s and the press pack accompanying the launch of each edition would include extensive back-up material including maps, photographs and video footage. The Soviet Union replied, in due course, with its regular publication, *Whence the Threat to Peace*, which described US military forces and strategy. Both publications were promoted abroad by the relevant information agencies.

High profile communication sources such as radio stations, press agencies and major reports are accompanied by a wide range of private briefings of opinion formers. Of immediate importance are newspaper, radio and television editors and correspondents, and politicians, but in the longer term particular attention is given to academics, especially those with an advisory role towards government. Information agencies select opinion formers to receive briefings which may take the form of extensive visits to the home country, at government expense. Such visits may not seek purely to reinforce sympathetic views, but will also be offered to those known to oppose a particular policy, in the expectation that exposure to the full context of the policy concerned will lead to a change or at least a moderation of the opinion.

Another common form of influence is to promote visits by specialists to the country concerned, often in the form of a lecture tour but supported by a press organisation adequate to ensure good coverage of the visit in the media. It may even be thought appropriate to engage the services of a

5. President's Advisory Committee on Information, *Sixteenth Annual Report to Congress*, US Government Printing Office, Washington, 1961, p. 3.

public relations organisation, although this is normally the response of a government with limited information facilities of its own.

One relatively recent development has been the growth of non-governmental organisations broadly supportive of a particular administration in the implementation of its foreign policy, or supportive of the more general aims of a formal or informal alliance. An example of the former in the US would be the Heritage Foundation, sympathetic to the foreign policy outlook of the Reagan administration and supportive of a number of overseas organisations broadly in sympathy with this outlook. The Heritage Foundation has been particularly active in Europe, especially in Britain, in the 1980s, with some concentration on issues of security and East–West relations.

In terms of the western alliance, an example of a loosely supportive organisation would be the Ditchley Foundation, which runs discreet seminars at Ditchley Park near Oxford in England. This brings together senior members of government and opinion formers to examine issues of mutual interest in a broadly Anglo-American context. Ditchley operates within the western security consensus and is an organisation more of influence than propaganda.

The value of the more propagandistic organisations, such as the Heritage Foundation, is that they may seek to exercise influence in a country in a manner which would be directly counter-productive if it was conducted by a government agency. Their activities may be of considerable value in promoting a particular foreign policy yet they can operate at a distance from government.

In summary, instruments of propaganda vary from the public to the private and from governmental through to quasi-independent organisations. A wide range of channels is available, and considerable resources can be devoted to achieving a shift in opinion.

Economic Weapons

The most commonly used weapons of economic influence in foreign policy are aid and trade. Foreign aid is, in practice, a widely used instrument of foreign policy, in both a positive and a negative sense. Much governmental aid is actually concerned with developing new markets for the exports from the donor or with enhancing existing markets. The recipient is thereby tied in economically with the donor country. More specifically, an aid package can be offered as a means of ensuring political sympathy with the donor, or an aid programme can be threatened if sympathy for a particular foreign policy objective is not forthcoming.

Most aid relationships imply major differences in wealth between the donor and recipient, with consequent power being the province of the former. Where this asymmetry is lacking, manipulation of trading relationships may replace aid as an instrument of foreign policy. Such manipulation may take several forms, the most extreme of which are normally boycotts and embargoes. A boycott involves the refusal to purchase particular commodities from the country concerned, whereas an embargo involves refusal to sell needed commodities. Both are used most commonly when interstate relations are already seriously impaired, and may even be a prelude to military intervention. Less extreme economic instruments include tariffs and quotas. Tariffs are routinely erected against imports for fiscal purposes and to protect home industries, but may be employed specifically to influence the behaviour of a trading state in some other political arena. Quotas involve agreements to allow imports of a set quantity of a commodity, usually at a favourable price, and quotas too can be adjusted for political purposes.

In addition to trade policies such as embargoes and tariffs, monetary policies, including credit facilities and currency transactions, can be employed, although both may require the exertion of influence on intergovernmental organisations.

The use of economic instruments of foreign policy is limited by three sets of factors. One relates to the dependency of the country being targeted. The ideal circumstances would be a small economy tied very closely to a much larger economy by close trading relationships, with the small economy being almost entirely dependent on the other, to the exclusion of other markets. The strong economy would, on the other hand, have readily available alternative sources of supply for imports and markets for exports. Such circumstances of dependency are rare, but unequal trading relationships are common in the case of a few major trading states such as the United States, Japan, West Germany and the United Kingdom. Even so, alternative markets may exist for the state being targeted, and may require the stronger state to seek informal agreements with allies to support its actions.

A second limitation relates to the fact that most strong trading states operate within what are broadly free markets. Consequently, the capacity for a state to engage in economic activities to the detriment of another may

57

have negative domestic consequences. Restricting imports or exports of particular goods will directly affect consumers and producers unless alternative sources and markets are available at no extra cost. The decision of the Carter administration to restrict grain sales to the Soviet Union in 1979 after the Soviet intervention in Afghanistan may have been reasonably well received in the United States as a whole, but was opposed by much of the farming lobby.

Finally, transnational corporations may be heavily involved in particular areas of trade which a government may seek to control. This may not be in the interest of the corporations concerned and they may have sufficient power to counter government intentions. Following the OPEC-inspired oil price rises of 1973–4, many analysts anticipated joint action by western governments and major oil companies. In practice the companies were able to manipulate the rapidly rising prices to their own advantage, buying low and selling high, and failed to co-operate successfully with governments. They were essentially independent actors in the world economy.

These three factors provide considerable limitations on the capacity of a state to exercise influence through economic means, unless the target state is particularly weak and isolated. It is therefore common for the state concerned to employ threats rather than action. The most effective threat can be made by suggesting that public opinion back home is likely to prove so strong that domestic action, especially in terms of boycotts of imports from the target state, is the likely eventuality. Such general threats, particularly if directed at the producing communities in the target state, can induce a feeling of vulnerability which can be a powerful asset in shifting public opinion.

Risks to Security

The brief survey of options given here indicates that a wide range of possibilities existed for the United States in mid-1984. They ranged from the usual methods of diplomatic bargaining through to efforts aimed at modifying opinion and even the use of direct threats of economic counter-measures. In the New Zealand case, however, there was the constant risk of adverse public reaction to apparently heavy-handed action by the United States, and it could therefore be expected that an effective form of pressure would be to suggest that New Zealand's own security was at risk.

In the case of a country within an alliance which takes action likely to affect that alliance, other members, and especially a leading member, are likely to counteract such a tendency by concentrating on security risks. Through all the usual channels, both official and unofficial, it is made clear that the action is a deviation from a norm which has maintained the security of the country. The risks involved can be heightened if it can be made clear that the new policy directly jeopardises particular security arrangements. The ultimate aim is therefore to give a clear impression that the actions being pursued will damage the country's security and increase its vulnerability. New Zealand was in this position within ANZUS, so the United States could be expected to focus on the damage which New Zealand might be doing to its own security.

For maximum effect, such a focus would require a degree of support from the other ANZUS partner, Australia. This could cause some problems, for Australia's Labour government, while essentially centre-right in political terms, had to contend with strong anti-nuclear sentiments within the country and party which would not be ready to accept Australian support for the United States in its policy towards New Zealand.

Even so, the United States also had to consider the problem of alliance solidarity within NATO. In this context, it was all too ready to raise questions of security with any NATO member which might appear to step out of line. If lack of solidarity in NATO could affect a country's security, then surely this could be said to apply to ANZUS as well. In the final analysis, the spectre of the Soviet threat might be the best issue to raise in seeking a more compliant government in Wellington.

CHAPTER 5

Labour in Office:
The First Six Months

As soon as the 1984 general election had been called by Robert Muldoon, the United States government wasted little time in making its feelings known on Labour's pledge to ban nuclear warships from New Zealand ports.

On 25 June, in a speech at Pennsylvania State University, the US State Department's Assistant Secretary for East Asian and Pacific Affairs, Paul Wolfowitz, argued that the United States attached 'critical importance' to the opportunity to use Australia and New Zealand ports which provided ready access to the South Pacific and Indian Oceans: 'We view Australia's and New Zealand's willingness to allow us use of their ports as part of their contribution to ANZUS.'[1] According to Geoff Kitney, writing in the Australian weekly *The National Times*, US officials in Wellington later claimed that Wolfowitz had planned to say something even stronger but had been persuaded to tone down his remarks.[2] Nevertheless, the United States Ambassador to New Zealand, H. Monroe Browne, released a copy of Wolfowitz's speech in Wellington together with a statement from the embassy drawing attention to his comments on port access for nuclear ships. David Lange complained to the US Embassy and a good many New Zealand voters shared his anger and resentment at this apparent outside interference in New Zealand politics.

1. Cited in Geoff Kitney, 'Why NZ Labour Scares Bob Hawke', *The National Times – Australia's National Weekly of Business and Affairs*, 20–6 July 1984.
2. Ibid.

The Americans, it appears, learnt little from this episode. Only a few days prior to the 14 July election, selected groups of Wellington journalists, academics, politicians (both Labour and National) and their support staff were chosen to attend private 'quizzing sessions' with two visiting US congressmen. The US Embassy in Wellington was quick to point out that their visit was scheduled well before Muldoon had called the 'snap' election – which seems likely – but there was clearly no desire on the part of the United States to cancel their trip.

The congressmen involved were Stephen Solarz (Democrat) from Brooklyn, New York, and Joel Pritchard (Republican) from Seattle, Washington State. Both sat on the 'House Foreign Affairs Sub-committee on East Asia and the Pacific' – Solarz as chairperson. It was claimed that they were visiting New Zealand on a low key fact-finding mission. Reporting on the 'invitation only' briefings, Murray McLaughlin of the *Dominion* newspaper wrote that one person was so disturbed by the threatening tone of the congressmen that he informed David Lange.[3] According to McLaughlin: 'A common thread of the congressmen's delivery was a pretty naked threat that the United States could impose some sort of trade sanctions to New Zealand's disadvantage if Mr Lange persisted with his party's policy.'[4] When confronted with the argument that the United States was again interfering in the New Zealand election, the Public Affairs Counsellor at the US Embassy in Wellington, Chuck Bell, retorted that the congressmen were merely reflecting the mood on Capitol Hill which he described as a 'protectionist lobby'.[5] Again, there is some truth in this claim, but it is hard to believe that the timing of their comments and their target audience was not entirely coincidental with the general election due to be held a few days later.

It appears that overall the Americans totally misread the strength of feeling against nuclear ship visits in New Zealand prior to the election; a fact borne out by the subsequent voting in which 64 per cent of the votes were cast for parties which campaigned to ban nuclear ships. There was also a good deal of uncertainty in the American camp with regard to Labour's policy in opposition and how this might be amended if the party won the general election. It was common knowledge that David Lange was not a keen advocate of the nuclear ships ban and had rather been pushed along on the issue by the centre-left of the party. Thus the

3. Murray McLaughlin, 'Lange's Nuclear Dilemma', *The Dominion*, 26 July 1984.
4. Ibid.
5. Ibid.

question that the Americans were asking was whether after a Labour victory New Zealand would really attempt to exercise sovereignty within ANZUS and begin to question the nuclear deterrent assumption on which the treaty had come to be based, or whether it was simply an aberration due to the 'left' getting its way whilst Labour was in opposition, and that the 'realities' of office would soon see the policy rectified to make it possible for warship visits to continue.

When Labour won the election, their declared foreign policy objectives included, in addition to the nuclear ships ban, a promise to legislate for a nuclear-free New Zealand, and the intention to sponsor a regional conference under United Nations auspices to promote a Nuclear Weapon Free Zone in the South Pacific.[6]

Within forty-eight hours of winning the election, David Lange was faced with major economic and foreign policy crises. The economic crisis was precipitated by outgoing Prime Minister Robert Muldoon who attempted to cling to the last vestiges of power for as long as possible. In direct conflict with constitutional convention, Muldoon refused to accept the advice of the Prime Minister-elect to devalue the NZ dollar by 20 per cent. Muldoon argued that Lange did not understand the realities of government. The outrage felt by Lange and his yet to be sworn-in government was fortunately shared by a majority of Muldoon's outgoing cabinet which forced him to implement the 20 per cent devaluation.

The foreign policy crisis, whilst not unexpected, was perhaps more immediate than Lange would have preferred. The 33rd ANZUS Council meeting was convened in Wellington on 16/17 July, just two days after Labour's victory at the polls, but before Lange had taken office. Lange faced anticipated heavy pressure from US Secretary of State George Shultz over the intention to stop the visit of nuclear ships. However, because of the timing of the ANZUS Council meeting New Zealand was to be represented by a minister from the defeated Muldoon government. Clever diplomatic footwork by Lange helped to diffuse this situation too. Although not required by protocol, Lange chose to fly down from Auckland to Wellington to meet Shultz when he arrived on New Zealand soil. This political gesture was commented on favourably by Shultz who said he was struck by the 'extraordinary courtesy' extended to him by the Prime Minister-elect.[7]

---

6. *1984 Policy Document (The Search for Peace)*, New Zealand Labour Party, Wellington, 1984.
7. Cited in Russell Dybvik, 'Air, Sea Access "Essential" to ANZUS Pact', *United States Information Agency Wireless File (Microtext Edition)*, East Asia/Pacific File 205 17 July 1984.

The subject of port calls by US nuclear warships did not come up for specific discussion at the ANZUS Council meeting, but in every other way it dominated the preceedings and was the main subject of the closing joint press conference by the ministers present.

The final joint communique of the Council meeting contained the statement that: 'Access by allied aircraft and ships to the airfields and ports of the ANZUS members was reaffirmed as essential to the continuing effectiveness of the Alliance.'[8] At the following press conference one reporter asked Shultz if it would mean the end of ANZUS if the Labour Party was to implement its nuclear ships ban, to which Shultz replied: 'Well, we will have to see what happens. . . . I think it is better to stay away from "iffy" questions, to state our positions clearly, and to work with the new government and see if we can't resolve the problem satisfactorily.'[9] But when asked if it was essential for United States Navy ships to be allowed into the ports of the ANZUS members, Shultz said: 'Of course . . . what kind of an alliance is it if the military forces of the countries involved are not able to be in contact with each other . . .'[10] In response to another questioner, Shultz said that there was no need to renegotiate the ANZUS Treaty – something which the Labour Party was pledged to do.[11] However, according to New Zealand political scientist Roderic Alley, there were some indications that Shultz was more accommodating in private talks with Lange on this matter than his public comments suggested.[12]

Recalling the pledge to ban nuclear ships by the Hawke government in Australia when it was first elected in 1983, Shultz declared that New Zealand would learn the values of the ANZUS alliance just as Hawke had

8. Communique of *Thirty-Third ANZUS Council Meeting, Wellington. July 16–17, 1984*, Page 1 Item 2.
9. Cited in Dybvik 'Air, Sea Access'.
10. Ibid.
11. In its 1984 policy document, the Labour Party set out the policies it would follow after gaining office. Under the chapter 'International Affairs Policy', and subsection titled 'The Search for Peace (ANZUS)', the policy document states that: 'The next Labour Government will re-negotiate the terms of our association with Australia and the United States for the purpose of ensuring the economic, social and political stability of the South East Asian and Pacific regions. The basic requirements of such an updated agreement will be: a). New Zealand's unconditional anti-nuclear stance; b). the active promotion of a Nuclear Weapons-Free South Pacific; c). the acceptance of absolutely equal partnership on all issues handled within the terms of the agreement and unanimous agreement on all decisions taken under those terms; d). an absolute guarantee of the complete integrity of New Zealand's sovereignty', *1984 Policy Document*. New Zealand Labour Party, Wellington, 1984, p. 50.
12. Roderic Alley, 'ANZUS Schmanzus', *New Outlook*, September/October 1984, pp. 37–8.

done, 'as it grew into the job of government'.[13] Quite what was meant by this is open to interpretation, but a background paper entitled 'US and New Zealand: Trouble Down Under' by the right-wing Heritage Foundation in the United States in November 1984 commented that: 'Because Washington considers port visits important to the strength of ANZUS, it is furnishing extensive information on nuclear issues to the Lange Government.'[14]

After leaving New Zealand for Honolulu, Shultz said that the US Ambassador to New Zealand, H. Monroe Browne, would cancel his month-long vacation and stay in New Zealand to allow him the chance to work closely with Lange in providing information he might need.[15] He also ruled out any retaliation against New Zealand exports by the Reagan administration if the Labour Party stuck to its policy. ANZUS, he said, was a military security alliance, not a trade agreement.[16]

Perhaps most significantly, Shultz gave Lange a pledge that no requests for port facilities for American warships or submarines would be issued for the next six months. Particularly with the benefit of hindsight, it is clear that Shultz believed that Lange – if not the Labour Party – could be persuaded to alter the nuclear-free policies sufficiently to allow port calls to continue.

If there was to be a six month hiatus on a military level between the United States and New Zealand, with no requests for port visits, the same cannot be said for the diplomatic, political, economic and media-inspired attention paid to the ANZUS crisis. Intense diplomatic negotiations took place between New Zealand and the United States, the exact nature of which remains confidential on both sides. Speculation that 'compromises' between New Zealand's nuclear ships ban and the neither-confirm-nor-deny policy of the United States were about to be reached, surfaced in the media from time to time but were ultimately without foundation. There are indications, however, that extensive efforts were made by New Zealand representatives to reach an agreement with the United States. Perhaps this is best exemplified by the concluding comments of David Lange to the

13. Quoted in Peter Bale, 'Nuclear Ship Visits Key to ANZUS: Shultz', *The Evening Post*, 18 July 1984.
14. Dora Alves, 'US and New Zealand: Trouble Down Under', *Asian Studies Center Backgrounder (No.18)*, The Heritage Foundation, Washington DC, 14 November 1984, p. 10.
15. Reported in *The Maui News*, 18 July 1984.
16. Reported in David Barber, 'Anzus Aftermath: Political Positions Amid Protocol', *National Business Review*, vol. 15, no. 27 (issue 585), 23 July 1984, p. 16.

Defence Commission of Enquiry[17] in New Zealand in August 1986. In response to criticism of the way that he had handled negotiations with the United States, Lange wrote: 'One day the story of how hard New Zealand worked for a settlement [of the ANZUS dispute] will be able to be told. At the moment I will not go beyond pointing out that it was the U. S., and not New Zealand, which called a halt to our efforts to reach an accommodation.'[18] In addition to this diplomatic and political activity, Labour's first six months in office saw a pattern of responses to the ships ban emerge which was to be repeated – with varying degrees of intensity and public profile – throughout the dispute.

George Shultz may have wanted time and patience to 'work at' the problem, but the United States media had no such reservations about launching attacks on the Labour government's nuclear-free intentions. For example, under the headline 'Wellington starts an ANZUS fuss', the *Washington Times* carried an article by Edward Neilan in which Lange was castigated for upsetting the 'super' relationship between New Zealand and the United States.[19] It also warned that: 'However popular it may be for Mr Lange to tweak Uncle Sam's nose on this issue, New Zealand's precarious economic situation gives him very little leverage against one of his country's most important trading partners.'[20]

In a similar vein, the *Wall Street Journal* published an editorial, 'The Kiwi Disease', in which they expressed condescending alarm that the Lange government did not look like modifying the ships-ban once it had 'adjusted to the responsibilities of real power'.[21] The problem it seemed was not so much the 'Kiwi disease' itself, but the threat that it might spread to other nations. Thus the disease needed to be contained and then cured by explaining to Lange that 'the consequences of his country's moral afflatus will be this: No Nukes, No defense treaty'.[22]

17. The Defence Commission of Enquiry was established by the Labour government in 1986. It was part of a series of public consultation exercises designed to find out public opinion on New Zealand's defence needs. The Enquiry's attempts at finding a public consensus on defence and security options for New Zealand largely failed, and the final report was criticised for ignoring, or at least misrepresenting, submissions to the Enquiry which had advocated genuinely alternative security options such as non-alignment, civilian based defence and neutrality.
18. Letter from D. Lange to F. H. Corner reprinted in *Defence and Security: What New Zealanders Want*, Report of the Defence Committee of Enquiry, July 1986. Government Printer, Wellington 1986, Addendum III, p. 4.
19. Edward Neilan, 'Wellington Starts an ANZUS Fuss', *The Washington Times*, 3 August 1984.
20. Ibid.
21. 'The Kiwi Disease' (Editorial), *The Wall Street Journal*, 22 August 1984.
22. Ibid.

In addition to the media's hostile reaction to New Zealand's new government, by the beginning of 1985 several other developments were underway which would attempt to undermine the nuclear ships ban and embarrass the Lange administration.

Between November 1984 and March 1985 three pro-nuclear think-tanks in the United States initiated studies on ANZUS and the nuclear ships ban. They were the Heritage Foundation and the Georgetown University Center for Strategic and International Studies (CSIS), both based in Washington, and the Pacific Forum, a Honolulu-based political research centre.

As was mentioned earlier, the Heritage Foundation report 'US and New Zealand: Trouble Down Under' was written by Dora Alves (who was also a member of the Georgetown University CSIS), and argued that if Lange continued to ban nuclear ships from New Zealand, ANZUS would be destroyed.[23] Alves had been due to visit New Zealand in August 1984 – sponsored by the USIA – but her trip was cancelled by the United States Embassy in Wellington because of the delicate political situation over the ANZUS dispute. Alves' paper for the Heritage Foundation was reportedly well received in the White House.[24]

Perhaps the most revealing and detailed think-tank report was that written for the Pacific Forum by retired United States admiral Lloyd Vasey and Professor Henry Albinski, director of Australian Studies at Pennsylvania State University. Their 'restricted distribution' report was 'leaked' to the media in New Zealand and Australia which of course had the effect of making it all the more newsworthy.[25]

Between 29 October and 11 November 1984, Vasey and Albinski visited New Zealand to 'interview a broad range of Australian and New Zealand elite opinion, and otherwise to assess the public mood in the two countries'.[26] The following extracts from their nineteen-page report titled *Pacific Forum: Australia – New Zealand Trip Report* are indicative of their stance and the conclusions they reached on how the ANZUS dispute and Lange government should be handled.

23. Alves, 'US and New Zealand'.
24. See David McKnight, 'Spooks, Think-Tanks Join the ANZUS Gold Rush', *The National Times* (Australia), 1–7 March 1985.
25. See Kate Coughlin, 'US Nuclear Probe Says Save Lange', *New Zealand Times*, 27 January 1985.
26. Lloyd R. Vasey and Henry S. Albinski, *Pacific Forum: Australia – New Zealand Trip Report*, published by the *Pacific Forum*, January 1985, p. 1.

New Zealand's general position could heighten anti-nuclear feeling far afield. . . . and act as a catalyst for some South Pacific countries to bar US vessels.[27]

Actual or perceived American backdown would entail massive loss of political credit, something a great power could ill afford.[28]

The New Zealand government needs time to sort out what, politically and opposite the United States, it can and cannot do.[29]

In New Zealand, *outlooks* have been shifting in ways that on balance are unhelpful to the United States. . . [30]

Given widespread New Zealand public feeling about nuclear matters and the government's political popularity, the government there would not be easily pressured. . . . A private and sympathetic approach would work best. . . . Prime Minister Lange is a moderate within his party, and worth protecting.[31]

The United States should review and as feasible improve upon its information and persuasion effort . . . in New Zealand.[32]

In addition to his activities for the Pacific Forum, Henry Albinski also sought to establish an 'educational exchange' between Pennsylvania State University and the Victoria University in Wellington. Under sponsorship of US\$50,000 from the USIA, Albinski proposed an annual exchange of six US/NZ academics for two to three month trips.[33] However, by February 1985 the proposal had failed, not least because of the critical press it had received in New Zealand (particularly concerning the political implications of the USIA sponsorship).

Although Albinski failed to establish his own academic think-tank, he was a prominent member of another set up by Ray Cline, a former deputy director of the CIA and Fellow at the Georgetown University CSIS, who

27. Ibid., p. 10.
28. Ibid., p. 14.
29. Ibid., p. 14.
30. Ibid., p. 16.
31. Ibid., p. 15.
32. Ibid., p. 17.
33. 'US Funding for Student Exchange Likely', *The Dominion*, 11 December 1984. See also Roger Foley, 'US Professor Seeks Link to Victoria', *New Zealand Times*, 10 February 1985.

since mid-1984 had been working with conservative New Zealand academics in an attempt to establish an ANZUS think-tank. In a different faculty of Georgetown (the Ethics and Public Policy Center) there already existed an operation backed by the USIA to the extent of US$200,000 with the task of promoting the views of Europeans who supported United States nuclear policy (vis-á-vis Cruise and Pershing missile deployments) and offsetting the views of the European peace movements.[34] The CSIS was to be the rough equivalent for the Pacific region – and concern itself specifically with ANZUS.[35] Members of the CSIS think-tank included Cline, Albinski and John Dorrance of the US State Department, and, in New Zealand, Bruce Larson, a right-wing activist, and Dalton West, an academic.[36] The establishment of the above think-tanks should, of course, be seen in part as regional examples of a global 'think-tank' phenomenon promoted by the Reagan administration and its political supporters from 1979, but this does not detract from their subtle (and sometimes not so subtle) attempts to influence New Zealand public and political opinion, and reverse the nuclear ships ban.

It was not only from US think-tanks that criticism of Labours' nuclear-free policies was coming. The USIA with increasing frequency sponsored lecture tours by American academics and arranged for them to speak at meetings of business people, foreign affairs institutes, academic seminars and other 'influential' gatherings. One of the first such visits after the 1984 election was that of Dr Rudolf Tolkes, Professor of Political Science at the University of Connecticut. In a speech in Wellington to the Institute of International Affairs, he argued that if New Zealand went ahead with its proposed ban on nuclear warships, the country would lose international credibility and undermine attempts at international nuclear disarmament. Furthermore, for Tolkes, the ban on nuclear warships visiting New Zealand seemed like an 'almost flippant whim'.[37]

Another recurrent theme in the attempts to change New Zealand public opinion on the ships ban has been the implicit threats of trade sanctions. These, too, increased in number and ferocity after the 1984 election.

34. Reported in *The National Times* (Australia), 9–15 November 1984; Cited in *Wellington Confidential*, no. 19, January 1985.
35. See, for example, *Wellington Confidential*, no. 19, January 1985. Robin Ramsay, 'How the US Tries to Subvert Lange', *END Journal*, Feb.–March 1987, pp. 16–18.
37. *Wellington Confidential*, no. 19, January 1985, p. 2.
38. See Deborah Hannan, 'Warship Ban Flippant – US Lecturer', *The Dominion*, 5 September 1984. Also 'US Lecturer Sees Nuke Ban as Soviet Win', *The Evening Post*, 5 September 1984.

On 19 September 1984 Texas congressman Kika de la Garza warned that an exclusive American agreement with New Zealand to safeguard exports of New Zealand dairy produce might not be renewed. The informal agreement meant that the United States would consult with New Zealand before selling off or dumping its excess dairy produce on the world markets. According to de la Garza: 'That agreement has now expired. I could not foresee another agreement like that if this matter of visitation of our military and naval forces is in question.'[38] In fact, de la Garza was carefully restrained in his remarks on the agreement and its possible non-renewal, but his guarded comments were nevertheless sufficient to send jitters through the New Zealand farming community, which in turn were fuelled by the reaction of the National Party spokespeople in New Zealand on the issue. For example, acting opposition leader of the time Jim McLay said: 'In the past we have asked the United States Government . . . for assistance and support in maintaining our access to American markets and we cannot thumb our nose at the United States in the foreign policy sense and expect that next time we ask for that assistance it will be forthcoming.'[39]

On 4 December 1984 there was the first indication that trade and ANZUS might become officially linked, when William Brock, President Reagan's special trade representative, was asked at a briefing meeting for journalists whether the United States would punish New Zealand by linking trade with those policies that the Americans did not like. Although he refused to answer the question specifically, Brock did say: 'I have never understood people who say there is no linkage. . . . You simply are defying human logic if you believe that countries don't take into account the actions of other countries as we look at our total relationships.'[40] Amidst this speculation over possible trade reprisals, the burgeoning think-tanks and media exhortations, David Lange embarked on his first overseas travel as Prime Minister.

A little over three weeks after his election victory Lange travelled to Papua New Guinea for a regional meeting of Asian and Pacific Commonwealth leaders. It was here that Australian Premier Bob Hawke made

38. Quoted in Richard Long, 'Secret Pact Links Trade With ANZUS', *The Dominion*, 20 September 1984.
39. Quoted in Patricia Herbert, 'No American Retaliation Feared – PM', *The Evening Post*, 21 September 1984.
40. Quoted in David Barber, 'At Issue: A Billion-Dollar Trade With US, Given Nuclear "Linkage"', *National Business Review* (NZ), vol. 15, no. 47 (Issue 606), 17 December 1984, p. 8.

clear his distaste for New Zealand's nuclear ships ban, saying that it would strain relations between Canberra and Wellington. He reiterated his feelings more forcefully in a letter sent to Lange in January 1985, in which he wrote that Australia did not accept that ANZUS could mean different things to different members.[41]

The publication of details of Hawke's letter to Lange by the Australian weekly newspaper *The National Times* provoked severe criticism of Hawke from both sides of the Tasman, and a pledge from New Zealand Deputy Prime Minister Geoffrey Palmer that New Zealand would not buckle from its anti-nuclear stance despite any 'friendly persuasion' from its allies.[42]

In September 1984 Lange travelled to New York to attend the General Assembly of the United Nations. During his stay he had talks with George Shultz and revealed that the United States would be forwarding its 1985 schedule of requests for port visits to New Zealand during December. Lange said that the schedule would be carefully considered by his government and that there would be further discussions with the United States.[43] Significantly, he also said: 'We must by the July [1985] ANZUS [Ministerial] council meeting have a firm position for a complete understanding of what role maritime forces will play in the defence of New Zealand pursuant to that alliance.'[44]

Thus Lange had set a date by which time he expected the ANZUS dispute either to be resolved, or the implications of the effects of his government's nuclear ships ban on it to be fully understood by all sides. Hence the stage was set for the first 'real' test of the promise to bar nuclear-powered and/or-armed warships from New Zealand ports.

41. Cited in Hyam Gold, 'Labour's First 300 Days', in idem (ed.), *New Directions in New Zealand Foreign Policy*, Benton Ross, Auckland, 1985, p. 3.
42. Quoted in 'We Wont't Buckle – Palmer: Hawke's "Friendly Persuasion" Rejected', *The Dominion*, 26 January 1985.
43. Reported in 'ANZUS Decision Expected Next July', *Auckland Star*, 26 September 1984.
44. Ibid.

CHAPTER 6

No Entry For the *Buchanan*

In anticipation of the United States forwarding its 1985 schedule for port visits to the Lange government in December 1984, the Coalition Against Nuclear Warships (CANWAR) – a Wellington-based pressure group – published a comprehensive list of all the nuclear-armed and -powered warships in the United States Navy.[1] The list was compiled from publicly available sources and upstaged the media debate over the likelihood of the United States requesting port facilities for nuclear warships in 1985.

With a US request imminent, speculation had been mounting that the Labour government was seeking to find a compromise with the United States to allow a ship visit to take place. Indeed, as we shall see later, it was clear that the United States believed that just such a compromise had been found. However, the publication of the list of United States Navy vessels which would be 'banned' if Labour was fully to adhere to its electoral pledges had the effect of forcing the government's hand on the issue. Indeed, it is arguably no exaggeration to say that the CANWAR list was a major reason for the government subsequently turning down the United States request for port facilities for the USS *Buchanan*.

On 21 January, New Zealand Deputy Prime Minister Geoffrey Palmer confirmed that New Zealand had received a request from the United States for a ship visit in March, to coincide with the *Sea Eagle I-85* ANZUS naval exercises in the Tasman Sea.[2] At this stage the exact identity of the

1. 'Nuclear-Armed and Nuclear-Powered US Navy Vessels', published by the Coalition Against Nuclear Warships (CANWAR), Wellington, 2 December 1984.
2. Reported in Bernard Lagan, 'Officials Check On US Ships Weaponry', *The Dominion*, 22 January 1985.

ship in question was not publicly known, but the *Sydney Morning Herald* reported on 21 January that the ship was not likely to be nuclear-powered, thus New Zealand's decision as to whether or not to admit it rested solely on the issue of whether it would be carrying nuclear weapons.[3]

Two days later, Geoffrey Palmer (who was acting Prime Minister at this time while David Lange was away visiting the Tokelau Islands) perhaps unwittingly hinted that it was indeed the case that the ship would not be nuclear-powered but would be capable of carrying nuclear weapons. Palmer also indicated that if a ship was *capable* of carrying nuclear weapons, this did not necessarily mean that it would be banned from New Zealand.[4] This set the alarm bells ringing in the peace movement and the Labour Party. CANWAR spokesperson Nicky Hager warned that the government would have a fight on its hands if it attempted to claim that a nuclear-capable warship was not carrying nuclear weapons when it visited New Zealand.[5]

On 25 January – as we have seen in the previous chapter – Australian Prime Minister Bob Hawke's letter to Lange (which had arrived two weeks earlier) was leaked to the press. Hawke indicated that Australia would want ANZUS renegotiated if New Zealand refused to change its policy of banning nuclear warships.[6]

Although Palmer vigorously denied that New Zealand was on the point of accepting the United States request for a ship visit, the ambiguity contained in a 'ban' which did not specifically include all nuclear-capable vessels was being exploited by the media and peace movement. Bruce Kohn writing in the *Evening Post* on 26 January reported that opinion was hardening in the Labour government that the policy of refusing entry to nuclear warships should encompass a blanket ban on all nuclear-capable naval vessels.[7] The reason for this was simple. It was clearly impossible – given the United States' position of neither confirming nor denying the presence of nuclear weapons on board its naval vessels – for the New Zealand government to decide with absolute certainty that an American warship or submarine would not be carrying nuclear weapons if it was capable of doing so.

3. Ibid.
4. Cited in Anthony Hubbard, 'The Sinking of the Buchanan', *The Dominion Sunday Times*, 29 March 1987.
5. Ibid.
6. See, for example, Dr John Beaglehole, 'New Zealand: the end of an era', *Pacific Defence Reporter*, April 1985, p. 8.
7. Bruce Kohn, 'Crisis Brink for ANZUS Relations', *The Evening Post*, 26 January 1985.

The New Zealand Ministry of Defence and the External Intelligence Bureau had been instructed to assess the nuclear capability of the American warship that New Zealand had been asked to accept for a visit, but the indications were that they could not reach any definite conclusions.[8]

Palmer acknowledged on 23 January that the United States had conveyed to New Zealand the name of the warship they wanted to send, but he refused to reveal this information to the press. Only after the Ministry of Defence and External Intelligence Bureau had concluded their investigations would the ship's identity be made public.[9] Hence uncertainty, speculation and educated guesses were the order of the day along with intense lobbying of Labour MPs to prevent any nuclear-capable ships being granted entry to New Zealand.

On 28 January Lange returned to Wellington from the Tokelaus and attended the cabinet meeting in the afternoon where it is believed that he proposed that the American warship be permitted to enter New Zealand since it would be *unlikely* to be carrying nuclear weapons. It is far from clear whether Lange truly believed that this proposal stood any chance of being passed by the cabinet, or indeed whether he supported it himself. It is quite possible that he was merely airing a proposal that had come from his advisors at the Ministry of Defence and External Intelligence Bureau. Either way, the cabinet threw the proposal out and in so doing surprised many senior New Zealand and American officials who believed that an 'informal compromise' had been reached on the dispute.[10]

The morning newspapers on 29 January reported that New Zealand's defence and intelligence officials had failed to establish conclusively if the warship request put forward by the United States would breach the government's nuclear weapons ban.[11] At a press conference the previous evening Lange said that he was seeking further information on the ship's nuclear capability from the US government. Whilst still declining to reveal the name of the ship, Lange did admit that it was not nuclear-powered. He also stated that the US policy of refusing to confirm or deny if nuclear weapons were carried on particular ships was proving difficult to accommodate with New Zealand's ban on the entry of nuclear weapons.[12]

---

8. See Hubbard, 'The Sinking of the Buchanan'.
9. Reported in Bernard Lagan, 'US Warship's Name Known', *The Dominion*, 23 January 1985.
10. See Hubbard 'The Sinking of the Buchanan'.
11. Reported in 'PM Still Doubtful on Warship Visit', *The Dominion*, 29 January 1985.
12. Ibid.

On the afternoon of 29 January Lange invited the US Ambassador to New Zealand, H. Monroe Browne, to his office and proposed that the United States send a different ship. From comments he made at a press conference after the meeting, Lange inadvertently revealed the identity of the class of ship he suggested the Americans send:

> REPORTER: I think the public is due an explanation as to why you are confident a vessel coming here is not carrying nuclear arms – we have to go on your say so that it is not carrying nuclear arms.
> LANGE: You don't have to go on my say so at all. But let me tell you this, there are navy vessels in the United States Navy which are modern recent fighting ships, which are clearly, unmistakably not nuclear-armed.[13]

Lange's reference to modern fighting ships that were unmistakably not nuclear-armed was interpreted by journalist and researchers almost certainly to be a reference to the *Oliver Hazard Perry DD7* class of guided missile frigates.[14] They were right, but when the *Dominion* and *Auckland Herald* published details of the proposal – referring by name to the *Oliver Hazard Perry*-class frigate – there was consternation both in the New Zealand Parliament and at the United States Embassy in Wellington that such information had been 'leaked'. It appears that Lange was unaware that it was he who had 'leaked' the information at his press conference. The effect of the 'leak' was to scuttle the possibility of a deal with the United States, who at this point felt betrayed on two grounds. Firstly, US officials firmly believed that they had struck a deal with their New Zealand counterparts whereby the original ship request would be accepted by New Zealand. Secondly, they did not expect details of Lange's proposal to send a different ship to be made public in the New Zealand media.

The following day (30 January) the US Ambassador issued a statement which was widely interpreted as a signal that the substitute ship proposal had been dismissed by Washington. The statement made no mention of Lange's proposal, merely saying that the United States was still awaiting the New Zealand government's decision on the original request. When asked if this statement from the United States indicated that New Zealand's new proposal had been rejected, Lange said: 'One could say that if

---

13. Cited in Bernard Lagan, 'Lange's New Offer To US On Warship', *The Dominion*, 30 January 1985.
14. Hubbard, 'The Sinking of the Buchanan'.

there had been a developing dialogue then that statement appeared to put an end to it.'[15]

The uncertainty that was prevailing over whether Lange was prepared to compromise on the nuclear ships ban, and the general picture of confusion that had emerged during the previous few days, led the anti-nuclear movement hastily to call for a march in Auckland to show support for the ships-ban policy. At just forty-eight hours notice 15,000 people marched in Auckland on the evening of 31 January,[16] an impressive indication of public reaction given the small population of New Zealand.

Earlier in the day Lange had received a standing ovation at the government caucus meeting for his handling of the ships issue, and after the meeting Lange dispelled most fears that he was about to renege on the ships-ban policy when he said: 'That policy prohibits within New Zealand the presence of nuclear weapons, and that policy is firm. It will be upheld.'[17]

On the morning of 1 February, Lange responded to the original US request for a port visit by a nuclear-capable vessel. Rather than an outright rejection of the request, his response to Washington amounted to a re-statement of the Labour government's firm non-nuclear stance.[18] Even so, it was sufficient to provoke a strong response from the US State Department. In an official statement, the Department said: 'Should the visit of the ship we have requested be denied, we would have to reconsider our participation with New Zealand in the March ANZUS *Sea Eagle* exercise. . . . More broadly we would also have to consider the implications for overall co-operation with New Zealand under ANZUS.'[9]

As the ball swung back to Lange's court, he in turn issued a statement re-affirming New Zealand's commitment to ANZUS and the country's historical association with the United States.[20] By this time, however, despite the diplomatic formalities and politeness, it was clear that the United States found New Zealand's position unacceptable. The Wellington-based *Evening Post* reported in an 'exclusive' on 4 February that the

---

15. Cited in Bernard Lagan, 'Lange Expected To Reject Warships', *The Dominion*, 1 February 1985.
16. See, for example, 'March Draws Thousands', *New Zealand Herald*, 31 January 1985.
17. Quoted in 'Government Set to Shut Door on US N-ship Visit', *New Zealand Herald*, 1 February 1985.
18. See Tony Garnier, 'Nuclear Policy Akin to Chinese Puzzle', *The Evening Post*, 4 February 1985.
19. Quoted in Hugh Nevill, 'Strong Response From Washington', *The Dominion*, 2 February 1985.
20. See Beaglehole, 'New Zealand: the end of an era', p. 10.

United States was seeking a 'clearcut response as to whether the nominated warship can or cannot come.'[21] The Americans wanted a definite 'yes' or 'no' reply. The reply amounted to a 'no', and on 5 February the United States released the name of the ship, the conventionally powered but nuclear-capable USS *Buchanan*, and announced that it would not be calling at New Zealand.[22]

This refusal to allow the USS *Buchanan* port facilities in New Zealand brought forth a stream of criticism from the United States, Britain and even Australia. The next two-and-a half years saw a campaign to undermine and ultimately overturn the nuclear ships ban and the nuclear-free policies of the Labour government. In the following chapters, these attempts will be documented in some detail.

---

21. Quoted in Garnier, 'Nuclear Policy Akin to Chinese Puzzle'.
22. See, for example, Beaglehole, 'New Zealand the end of an era', p. 10.

CHAPTER 7

Post - *Buchanan*:
The Pressures Intensify

The responses to the refusal by New Zealand to allow the USS *Buchanan* port facilities were apparent at several levels. Firstly, there was the 'official' reaction, mainly from Washington, but to an extent also from Canberra. London and elsewhere. This included high-profile military reprisals by the United States in the form of a reduction in intelligence information, the cancellation of joint military exercises and exchanges, and the loss of status from that of an 'ally' to a 'friend'. In addition, there were also expressions of opposition to the New Zealand decision by other leaders around the world. Secondly, there were the threats of trade sanctions against New Zealand by Congressmen and Senators in the United States. Thirdly, one can identify the media reactions (both foreign and domestic) to the ships-ban. As we shall see, editorial writers had a field day rebuking New Zealand and in particular Lange. Finally, there was the domestic reaction in New Zealand to the port denial. The National Party Opposition and their supporters pitched in with warnings of dire consequences for New Zealand and ANZUS if the ships-ban continued.

It should be noted that whilst these various levels and types of response were probably not *coordinated* in their entirety (in the sense of some master plan directed from the White House, Pentagon or wherever), they were *complementary* in so far as they amounted to an enormous combined pressure on the New Zealand government to alter its stand, and perhaps more importantly, served as a warning to other US allies not to be

79

tempted to follow New Zealand's nuclear-free path.

Firstly then, we will examine the official reaction to New Zealand's ban on the USS *Buchanan*.

February – March 1985 : The 'Official' Reaction

If the Reagan administration had been following a policy of quiet diplomacy with the Lange government, the *Buchanan* incident abruptly ended it. On 5 February the Americans withdrew from the ANZUS *Sea Eagle I–85* naval exercises of which the *Buchanan* was to have been a part. It was left to Australian Premier Bob Hawke officially to cancel the exercises.

The cancellation of the *Sea Eagle I–85* exercises was to be the first in a series of punitive measures taken against New Zealand by the United States. In Washington the State Department said that it 'deeply regretted' the New Zealand decision (to ban the *Buchanan*), and an unnamed spokesperson said that 'appropriate responses' were being considered in co-ordination with other United States government agencies including the Pentagon, the Central Intelligence Agency and the National Security Council.[1]

The US position was that New Zealand's policy was incompatible with its obligation under ANZUS – something that New Zealand hotly denied – and US Defense Secretary Caspar Weinberger warned that: 'At the moment they [New Zealand] are following a course that can only be of great harm to themselves.'[2] One United States official was apparently so angered by the ships-ban that he declared New Zealand to be 'a piss-ant little country south of nowheresville',[3] but he was the exception rather than the rule (at least publicly) and other responses were still couched in the pleasantries of diplomatic language. However, one of the more explicit admissions of the reasoning behind the reaction of the United States was given by State Department spokesperson Bernard Kalb: 'Some Western countries have anti-nuclear and other movements which seek to diminish defense cooperation among the allied states. We would hope that our response to New Zealand would signal that the course these movements advocate would not be cost-free in terms of security relationships with the

---

1. Quoted in 'ANZUS: And then there were two', *Sydney Morning Herald*, 6 February 1985.
2. Quoted in 'Washington Warns Its Allies', *Macleans*, 18 February 1985, p. 29.
3. Quoted in Michael McKinley, 'Labour, Lange and Logic: An Analysis of New Zealand's Anzus Policy', *Australian Outlook*, vol. 39, no. 3, 1985, pp. 133–8.

United States.'[4]

Plans by the United States Congress to hold hearings to examine New Zealand's nuclear policy were reported in the Australian *National Times* on 8 February.[5] The head of the United States Congressional Sub-committee on East Asian and Pacific Affairs, Stephen Solarz, said that the hearings would be held in April or May.[6] In fact, they were held much earlier, on 18 March, and are described in detail shortly.

The dust had barely settled after the *Sea Eagle* cancellation, when the United States also called off a visit to US Military Headquarters in Hawaii by the New Zealand Parliamentary Defence Committee.[7] Then it was reported that the United States had withdrawn an invitation for a New Zealand *Orion* patrol plane to participate in anti-submarine exercises off Hawaii.[8]

On 18 February the United States withdrew at the last minute from an ANZUS military communications meeting due to be held in Sydney. A seminar leading up to the meeting was also cancelled.[9] In the wake of these American reprisals David Lange told reporters that he expected more 'embarrassment' from the United States. According to Lange, the Americans would not 'pull the rug' on New Zealand, but might 'polish the lino a bit harder in the hope that I execute a rather unseemly glide across it.'[10]

There could be little doubt that the lino was indeed being polished. On 20 February two more military exercises were cancelled by the United States. Firstly, there was the withdrawal of an invitation to the *Team Spirit* exercise due to be held in South Korea from 8 March.[11] Then followed the cancellation of the *Roll Call* exercise in Fiji and Australia for the autumn.[12] Although the Americans gave no official reason for the cancellation of *Roll Call*, the Wellington *Evening Post* had no hesitation in concluding that it was '[the] latest United States initiative to pressure New Zealand into lifting its ban on the entry of nuclear ships to its ports.'[13]

4. Quoted in Ted Galen Carpenter, 'Pursuing A Strategic Divorce: The US and the Anzus Alliance', paper written for the *CATO Institute* (Policy Analysis), no.67, 27 February 1986, p. 9.
5. Marian Wilkinson, 'Congress Hearings Planned on NZ No-Nuke Policy', *The National Times* (Australia), 8–14 February 1985, p. 8.
6. Ibid.
7. See Carpenter, 'Pursuing a Strategic Divorce', p. 3.
8. 'New Zealand Premier Reports New US Moves – Reaction to Ship Ban Continues', *Washington Post*, 20 February 1985.
9. 'Another Anzus "No"', *The Evening Post*, 19 February 1985.
10. Quoted in 'More Retaliation Expected by PM', *The Evening Post*, 19 February 1985.
11. Reported in 'More Military Events Cancelled – Prime Minister Low Key', *The Evening Post*, 20 February 1985.
12. Ibid.
13. Ibid.

The stern and uncompromising response to the ships-ban in Washington was not without its critics in the United States. For example, former Democratic Congressman Otis Pike wrote of the United States reactions: 'To show how really tough we are, there have been hints of withholding military intelligence from New Zealand and unleashing our mountains of surplus dairy products to devastate the New Zealand economy. . . . We do not stand tall by bullying the likes of New Zealand.'[14] However, any such criticism fell largely on deaf ears. United States officials (again unnamed) declared that the pattern of cancellations and postponements of joint military exercises with New Zealand would continue, 'probably for many months or even years until New Zealand changes its nuclear policy'.[15]

Secretary of State George Shultz said that New Zealand had 'basically taken a walk' from the ANZUS alliance, and in an address to the United States Senate Budget Committee he argued that the New Zealand ships-ban had changed the meaning of the ANZUS alliance, and made it inoperative as far as New Zealand was concerned.[16] Although Shultz cautioned against over-reaction to the ships-ban by the US Congress, he still felt sufficiently perturbed by events himself to say: 'We believe that those who live by freedom and benefit from freedom ought to be willing to defend it, so we're disappointed in that aspect of the New Zealand performance.'[17] At the same time as Shultz's address to the Senate Budget Committee, it was reported that when Lange stopped off in California en route to Britain on 25 February he would be met by Deputy Assistant Secretary of State William A. Brown – a relatively low-level greeting, and widely interpreted as a snub to Lange.[18]

David Lange left New Zealand on 25 February for talks with Brown in the United States, before travelling on to Britain for talks with Margaret Thatcher and to take part in the Oxford Union Debate, and thence to Geneva for the United Nations Conference on Disarmament. After a cabinet meeting just prior to his departure from New Zealand, Lange gave his firmest assurance that he was not about to compromise on the nuclear ships ban when he told reporters: 'This Government has a policy. That policy is not to have nuclear weapons in New Zealand. Now you don't

14. Otis Pike, 'ANZUS Row: "Pentagon Shooting US in Foot"', *The Evening Post*, 20 February 1985.
15. Quoted in Don Oberdorfer, 'US Rebuffs New Zealand – Military Exercises Canceled or Put Off', *Washington Post*, 21 February 1985.
16. Anthony Hubbard, 'Shultz Tell Congress Not to Over-React', *The Dominion*, 21 February 1985.
17. Quoted in ibid.
18. Oberdorfer, 'US Rebuffs New Zealand'.

compromise on that. You don't have them half in New Zealand. You don't have them sometimes in New Zealand. . . .'[9]

When Lange met William Brown in Los Angeles he was told more fully of the American measures which would be taken against New Zealand in the wake of the *Buchanan* refusal. Reciprocal visits by senior military staff would be put off, and New Zealanders training in US defence establishments would finish their terms but not be replaced.[20] More ominously perhaps, several categories of intelligence information would no longer be provided to New Zealand. The rationale for this was that although US officials still considered New Zealand to be a 'friend' of the United States, its status as an 'ally' was not so certain. The sharing of intelligence, it seems, was conditional on allied status.[21]

Back in Wellington, Deputy Prime Minister Geoffrey Palmer called the US reprisals 'extremely harsh' and an 'over-reaction'.[22] He added: 'The fact that the measures have undoubtedly been taken to make a point to other allies in Western Europe and elsewhere cuts no ice with this Government.'[23] Speaking in Los Angeles to a meeting of the New Zealand Connection (a business persons club with strong New Zealand links), Lange reacted angrily to the American moves to isolate and embarrass his government. For the first time, he suggested that the United States government strategy appeared to be aimed at changing the government in New Zealand: 'The undeclared strategy of the United States appears to be to curtail its long-established defence relationship with New Zealand till such time as a Government is elected which will admit American nuclear weapons.'[24]

A day later, after arriving in London for talks with Prime Minister Margaret Thatcher, and to participate in the Oxford Union Debate, Lange was just as vehement in his anger at the United States. The US actions to scale down its co-operation with New Zealand in defence and intelligence fields were, he said:

Designed to embarrass us, to cause morale in the defence force to be

19. Quoted in Richard Long, 'Lange off With Message: "We're No Client State"', *The Dominion*, 26 February 1985.
20. Reported in Anthony Hubbard, '"A Serious Disagreement" – US Action Branded Extremely Harsh', *The Dominion*, 28 February 1985.
21. See, for example, Carpenter, 'Pursuing a Strategic Divorce'.
22. 'Retaliation by US Harsh, Palmer Tells Parliament', *The Evening Post*, 28 February 1985.
23. Ibid.
24. Quoted in Richard Long, 'Lange – Our Role is Diminished', *The Dominion*, 28 February 1985.

affected. . . . The leader of the Opposition [National Party leader Jim McLay] has already declared his commitment to snuggling up to the bomb, and I have no doubt that various efforts will be made [by the US] to keep that course on track. . . . The type of pressure which large powers can exert over small ones is seen. . . as being somewhat akin to the very totalitarianism we are supposed to be fighting against.[25]

At this stage of the arguments over repercussions, reprisals and ANZUS obligations, the British had been largely conspicuous by their silence on the matter. It was no secret that the Thatcher government took a dim view of New Zealand's actions, but there was not the same expression of absolute outrage from London as there clearly was in Washington. This is understandable given that ANZUS does not involve Britain directly, but it was also apparent that New Zealand's nuclear ships ban would apply to the vessels of the Royal Navy which also operate under a neither-confirm-nor-deny policy. Clearly, the British believed that a compromise would be agreed on by Lange's government before Britain became embroiled in the dispute.

Lange in Europe

In his discussions with Prime Minister Margaret Thatcher, it was made clear to Lange that Britain stood firmly with the United States on the nuclear ships ban, but the British response was generally far more low key, and talks between the two leaders focused in great measure on Britain's continued support for New Zealand in the forums of the European Economic Community.

After meeting Thatcher, Lange participated in an internationally tele-vised Oxford Union Debate on 1 March. In the debate – 'This house believes that nuclear weapons are morally indefensible' – Lange was the main speaker for the affirmative, and opposite him, speaking for the negative, was the US Moral Majority leader the Rev. Senator Jerry Falwell.

The pairing of a Prime Minister and a right-wing church leader to take part in the debate was arguably a little odd, but both Lange and Falwell are eloquent, persuasive speakers and Lange had once been a Methodist lay preacher. The ensuing debate was one of the most closely followed for many a year at Oxford. For his part, Lange was afforded a hitherto

25. Quoted in 'Lange Suggests Washington Ouster', *The Evening Post*, 1 March 1985.

unprecedented standing ovation both before and after his main speech. During the debate, Lange first spoke of the inherent insecurity engendered by nuclear weapons – whatever the *intention* of their deployment: 'A system of defence serves its purpose if it guarantees the security of those it protects. A system of nuclear defence guarantees only insecurity. . . . The intention of those who for honourable motives use nuclear weapons to deter is to enhance security; they succeed only in enhancing insecurity.'[26] Specifically on justifying his country's nuclear-free policies, Lange said:

> It makes no sense for a country which faces no threat to seek to surround itself with nuclear weapons. It makes no sense for that country to ask its allies to deter enemies which do not yet exist with the threat of nuclear weapons. It makes no sense for a region which is the most stable in the world to allow itself to become a strategic arena for the nuclear powers.[27]

And on the US response to the ships-ban:

> We have been told by officials in the United States Administration that our decision is not . . . to be cost free; that in fact we are to be made to pay for our action. Not by our enemies, but by our freinds. We are to be made an example of; we are to be ostracised and anathematised until we are compelled to resume our seat in the dress circle of the nuclear theatre. . . . We are actually told that New Zealanders cannot decide for themselves how to defend New Zealand but are obliged to adopt the methods which others use to defend themselves. . . .[28]

If the US government thought that Lange might rescind the ships-ban and come running back to the nuclear fold, then the Oxford debate must have been a rude awakening. What was perhaps especially interesting, was the vigour with which Lange defended the policy – and castigated New Zealand's so-called ally – when less than a year earlier it was known that he was doubtful about the policy himself. It is possible that over the months Lange had genuinely changed his mind or that he supported the policy only because it was politically expendient to do so (given the widespread popular support it commanded in New Zealand). But it is also extremely probable that the 'heavy handed' US response did little to

26. Quoted in 'Nuclear Policy Sparks Debate', *New Zealand Foreign Affairs Review* (Ministry of Foreign Affairs, Wellington), vol. 35, no. 1, January – March 1985, p. 8.
27. Ibid., pp. 9–10.
28. Ibid., p. 10.

engender support for their cause with the New Zealand Prime Minister.

Lange concluded his forceful speech to the Oxford Union by declaring that there was no humanity in the logic which argued that New Zealand must be obliged to play host to nuclear weapons because other countries in the West did so. In Lange's words: 'It is a self-defeating logic. . . . To compel an ally to accept nuclear weapons against the wishes of that ally is to take the moral position of totalitarianism, which allows for no self-determination.'[29]

In Geneva, Lange was the first ever head of government to address the UN Conference on Disarmament, and the message he delivered was essentially the same as that in Oxford, but he also concentrated on the progress of arms control – which he described as 'bleak' – and the part that small nations could play in it. New Zealand, by its action in banning nuclear weapons from its territory, had, he argued, 'applied a limited measure of arms control'.[30] In addition, New Zealand had been instrumental in supporting the proposal adopted by the South Pacific Forum for the establishment of a South Pacific Nuclear Free Zone, and had promoted a United Nations General Assembly resolution on a Comprehensive Test Ban. He also emphasised the New Zealand position with regard to ANZUS, which maintained that the alliance was a *conventional* one: 'New Zealand is a member of the ANZUS alliance because we see its usefulness as a conventional alliance to us and to our region. . . . If ANZUS were purely a nuclear alliance, then there would be no point in New Zealand staying in it.'[31]

However, it was at his speech in Geneva that Lange also made a controversial statement that New Zealand's action in banning nuclear vessels from its waters was not intended to be 'exported' around the world:

> The people and Government of New Zealand have rejected participation in the nuclear arms race. We do not say to any country in the world, do as New Zealand does; all we say is that when the opportunity is given to any country to pursue a serious and balanced measure of arms control, then that country has a duty to all of us to undertake that measure.[32]

As we shall see, this denial that New Zealand was setting an example for

29. Ibid., p. 11.
30. Ibid., p. 12.
31. Ibid., p. 13.
32. Ibid., p. 17.

others to follow was to cause controversy among Lange's cabinet colleagues, and criticism from the peace movement.

More US Reprisals

While Lange was still in Britain, it was reported that officials of the Reagan administration had drawn up proposals to exclude New Zealand from another ANZUS meeting scheduled for late March or early April.[33] Furthermore, in Australia the Federal cabinet were discussing the future of the ANZUS Treaty amidst growing speculation that the annual ANZUS Council meeting, due to be held in July, would be cancelled. It transpired that the US authorities were in no doubt that the meeting should be cancelled or postponed, but that they wanted the notice of cancellation to come from Australia. The *Sydney Morning Herald* reported that US Secretary of State George Shultz put the proposal (to cancel the meeting) to Australian Prime Minister Bob Hawke at a meeting in Washington during February, with the intention of thus forcing Australia to abandon the largely 'non-interventionist' stance on the dispute that it had so far taken.[34]

Accordingly, on 5 March Bob Hawke postponed indefinitely the annual ANZUS Council meeting on the grounds that since the US would refuse to attend while New Zealand's nuclear ships ban remained, there would be little point in holding the meeting. Hawke declared that the ANZUS Treaty, whilst still existing as a trilateral agreement, did so 'in name only, with virtually nothing of it operative now'.[35] The *New York Times* reported that had it not been for the pressure from Shultz, Hawke would not have postponed the meeting.[36] In London David Lange responded to the postponement by also claiming that Australia had made the decision at the 'behest of the United States', adding: 'Apparently the United States is now turning the rack a degree further.'[37]

True to form, a number of 'unnamed sources' in the United States were

33. 'US Wants NZ Out: Officials', *The Evening Post*, 4 March 1985.
34. Cited in Richard Long, 'ANZUS Talks Called Off – Treaty Exists in Name Only', *The Dominion*, 5 March 1985.
35. Quoted in 'US – New Zealand Rift Causes Postponement of ANZUS Pact Meeting', *Los Angeles Times*, 5 March 1985.
36. Bernard Gwertzman, 'Meeting of ANZUS Alliance Is Postponed', *The New York Times*, 5 March 1985.
37. Quoted in Peter O'Hara, 'US "Turning the Rack" Says Lange', *The Dominion*, 5 March 1985.

quick to offer explanations for the postponement, one of which (a 'State Department official') was reported in the *New York Times* as saying: 'We are trying to turn the New Zealand decision around . . . and we cannot allow the impression to be created that we are willing to overlook the port call question.'[38] And with an impressive line in 'doublespeak' the same 'official' continued: 'We are not asking New Zealand to accept nuclear weapons. . . . We only want him [sic] to allow the ships to call without our saying whether they have nuclear weapons or not, just as we do in countries all around the world.'[39]

Coincidental with the announcement from Canberra of the ANZUS Council meeting postponement, the US Ambassador to New Zealand, Mr H. Monroe Browne, speaking to the Hawera Presbyterian Men's Fellowship in New Zealand on 5 March, accused the Lange government of walking away from a system of defence co-operation developed under ANZUS over many years: 'We can only conclude that New Zealand's decision not to participate in certain aspects of defence co-operation means that your Government is no longer willing to share the full burden of defence with Australia and the United States. . . .'[40] Browne's speech, which was widely reported, provoked an angry reaction from acting Prime Minister Geoffrey Palmer who called the statements from Browne 'false and misleading',[41] and said: 'Far from walking away from a defence system, as the ambassador says, New Zealand is being kicked around. It is not pleasant. . . . The New Zealand Government does not see why "solidarity" in an alliance always means agreeing with the American view. . . .'[42]

It was not only Mr Monroe Browne who was spreading the US message around New Zealand. The *National Business Review*, for example, reported that businesses in Dunedin were being visited by an economist from the United States Embassy in Wellington warning of dire consequences for New Zealand exports if the ships-ban continued.[43]

One day after the Monroe Browne incident, a bitter row erupted in the New Zealand Parliament when one of Lange's senior ministers, Richard

38. Quoted in Gwertzman, 'Meeting of ANZUS Alliance Is Postponed'.
39. Ibid.
40. Quoted in Bernard Lagan, 'Palmer Hits Out At American Diplomat', *The Dominion*, 6 March 1985.
41. Ibid.
42. Ibid.
43. Sharyn Steel, 'Visits From US Embassy Press Nuclear Line'. *National Business Review*, vol. 16, no. 8 (issue 614), 11 March 1985, p. 3.

Prebble, launched a scathing attack on Opposition leader Jim McLay. Prebble alleged that McLay had an interest in seeing the US retaliatory measures carried out, since his political credibility rested on such actions being taken. And he argued that McLay had received a great deal of information on the ANZUS issue, 'some of which had not been made available to Her Majesty's Government'.[44] Labour's chief whip, Dr Michael Cullen, entered the fray when he accused McLay of advising the American government on ways to de-stabilise New Zealand.[45] For his part, McLay denied the accusations, but it does appear that he knew of the *Sea Eagle* cancellation several days before the announcement was made by the United States government.[46]

It was also in March that an attempt was made to persuade the Americans to encourage a higher British profile in the ships-ban row. The attempt was made by former Australian Prime Minister Malcolm Fraser, who on 7 March wrote a private letter to then US Vice President George Bush. It was never intended that the letter be published, but in 1986 it was leaked to the media, and Fraser's advice to Bush was revealed for all to see.[47] In it Fraser was emphatic in his support for the American position, but he felt that the ANZUS Treaty was in danger of collapse if it was perceived that the United States was 'bullying' New Zealand. Fraser argued that it was essential to preserve the fabric of ANZUS, even if only for its symbolism.[48] In order for this to happen, Fraser wrote: 'The time has come, I believe, for a significant change of emphasis in the conduct of the dispute. . . .'[49] This 'significant change' meant using Britain to tug at a few colonial heartstrings – principally by requesting a port visit by a Royal Navy vessel. To refuse port facilities for a ship from the 'mother country' would alienate much support for the government, Fraser believed. In his own words:

> I am sure that most New Zealanders do not realise that their Government's policy includes visits from Royal Navy vessels . . . the time is now right for a different approach which will offer greater prospects of

44. Quoted in Brian Woodley, 'Gvt Assault on McLay Led Earlier by PM, Prebble', *The Evening Post*, 7 March 1985.
45. 'Loyalty Questioned: McLay Attacked Over US "Talks" and "Advice"', *The Evening Post*, 7 March 1985.
46. Ibid.
47. 'The ANZUS Plot: Fraser's Advice to Yanks on how to Knobble Lange', *New Zealand Monthly Review*, April 1987, pp. 7–8.
48. Ibid.
49. Ibid.

achieving the kind of change in attitude in New Zealand that we would all want. . . . New Zealand has always felt closer to Britain than to Australia or the United States. It is a relationship that should be used to the full on this issue.[50]

And Fraser continued:

Even if Britain is reluctant, I would have thought there were ways in which Britain could be persuaded to participate in a resolution of the issue. . . . British influence, properly used, can be pre-eminent in achieving a change of heart in New Zealand, and the tragedy is that that approach has not been adopted low key, and long ago. . . .[51]

It would, of course, be naive to suggest that one letter alone changed the US approach, but Bush was clearly impressed with the Fraser message. In a reply to his letter (again leaked) Bush said: 'I received your extraordinarily interesting letter and will hold it very, very closely. I don't feel comfortable commenting on it here for the reasons you cited in your letter, but I just want you to know that I was very grateful for the Fraser insight.'[52] And, perhaps not entirely by coincidence, the British did indeed adopt a higher profile in the dispute from May 1985 onwards. It is impossible to prove that Fraser's letter was influential in this respect, but, if nothing else, it is interesting in so far as it provides an example of the 'behind the scenes' attempt to undermine the Labour government in New Zealand.

In fact, the first signs of British involvement in the ships-ban dispute were reported on 13 March, when British officials in London were said to be 'mulling over' a proposed warship visit to New Zealand in 1986.[53] The New Zealand High Commissioner in London, Joe Walding, commented that both countries would have to 'work very hard' to resolve the differences between them, particularly because Britain, like America, refuses as a matter of policy to disclose whether its warships are carrying nuclear arms.[54]

One other interesting development in late March was a report in the New Zealand press saying that Washington had given Lange top-secret

50. Ibid.
51. Ibid.
52. Ibid.
53. 'Brit Ship Visit Poses Problems', *The Evening Post*, 13 March 1985.
54. Ibid.

advice that the USS *Buchanan* would not be carrying nuclear weapons when it visited New Zealand. Asked at a press conference if this assertion was true, Lange replied: 'No it is not, quite emphatically not, and I was not in the position where I received any such assurance. I was in fact specifically told that no such assurance could be given.'[55]

Lange's denials did little to dampen the anger of many US officials who felt that they had been misled by their New Zealand counterparts into believing that the *Buchanan* would be accepted. One official said the United States had been caught off guard by the *Buchanan* refusal: 'We had hoped and indeed expected that the ship would be accepted.'[56]

The reactions to the refusal to permit the USS *Buchanan* port facilities in New Zealand were not confined to the official announcements and retaliatory measures from Washington, nor to the private correspondence between Malcolm Fraser and George Bush. There were increased calls for trade sanctions and other economic reprisals against New Zealand, a proliferation of media editorials castigating the New Zealand action, and the beginning of intense efforts in New Zealand to have the ships-ban reversed. It is to these other reactions to the ships-ban that we now turn.

February – March 1985: The Threatened Trade Backlash

The implicit threat of trade sanctions against New Zealand in the light of the nuclear ships ban policy was arguably a more effective means of reversing New Zealand's policy than the military reprisals which the United States and Australia were undertaking. In a country with such a narrow economic base, and so dependent on the American and European markets for its meat and dairy products, any suggestion that these markets might be closed down (or flooded with North American or EEC surpluses in the same products) is guaranteed to cause grave concern to the farming and business communities and the politicians.

We have seen already that in the opinion of some United States Congressmen and Senators ANZUS and trade were linked – albeit informally. Following the refusal to allow the USS *Buchanan* port facilities, the threat of trade reprisals gained a higher profile in the dispute.

On a matter so fundamental to New Zealand's livelihood and prosperity, any moments of light relief were to be savoured, and one such

55. Quoted in Richard Long, 'Lange Rejects Advice Claim', *The Dominion*, 22 March 1985.
56. Quoted in 'US "Caught off Guard"', *The Evening Post*, 7 March 1985.

moment occurred towards the end of January, when Australia's Queensland State Premier, Sir Joh Bjelke-Peterson, decided to teach New Zealand a lesson with his own trade sanctions. Sir Joh, a New Zealander by birth and a man of firm right-wing views, ordered that a shipment of chocolates from Auckland be held in Brisbane ostensibly because they did not meet Queensland labelling requirements. But by his own admission, Sir Joh impounded the chocolates to demonstrate the 'silliness' of New Zealand's anti-nuclear politics: 'I don't expect our action will make the New Zealand Government change its mind but at least it will highlight their naive nuclear policies.'[57]

Back in October 1984 Sir Joh had called on the Australian government to impose higher tariffs on New Zealand goods to teach David Lange's government its 'ANZUS obligations'. He also predicted that New Zealanders would live to rue the day they elected a Labour government, and claimed that New Zealand was looking 'very stupid' and that the whole world was watching.[58]

If Sir Joh was proving to be an embarrassment to the Australians, and an amusement to most New Zealanders over his sabre-rattling protestations, his choice of banning chocolates was a god-send to headline writers in the New Zealand media. 'Sir Joh Drops Choc Bomb',[59] 'Chocs Away, It's Acid Drops',[60] and 'NZ Soft Centres in Sticky Chocolate Argument',[61] were just a few of the headlines which must have brightened many a breakfast table. But although Sir Joh was an easy target of ridicule, the same could not be said of those Senators and Congressmen in the United States who yielded a far greater power and influence.

New Zealand Trade Minister Michael Moore warned the Labour cabinet – before the decision to bar the *Buchanan* had been taken – that possible American reprisals would extend beyond the military area. The *Financial Times* in London speculated that the United States might retaliate forcibly by making an 'example' of New Zealand to other allies contemplating anti-nuclear policies.[62] It was suggested that the United States could undertake trade reprisals in several areas:

57. Quoted in Bernard Lagan, 'Trade Row Erupts Over Nuclear Ban', *The Dominion*, 28 January 1985.
58. Quoted in 'Sir Joh Labours to Fulfill Prophecy', *The Dominion*, 29 January 1985.
59. 'Sir Joh Drops Choc Bomb', *Auckland Star*, 26 January 1985.
60. 'Chocs Away, It's Acid Drops', *New Zealand Herald*, 28 January.
61. 'NZ Soft Centres in Sticky Chocolate Argument', *New Zealand Herald*, 29 January.
62. Dai Hayward, 'New Zealand Takes the Threat of US Trade Retaliation Seriously', *Financial Times* (London), 7 February 1985.

— The withdrawal of administration opposition in Congress to legislation attempting to restrict New Zealand's agricultural imports to
the United States.

— The withdrawal of support for New Zealand butter sales in third
countries. Where the United States exported large quantities of
butter to a country where New Zealand also had a market, it had
previously insisted that the country still brought a quantity from
New Zealand.

— By a reduction in the quota of New Zealand beef imported into the
United States, replacing it with other suppliers.

— By dumping United States butter surpluses on the world market at
below the world minimum price.

— By exerting its influence in Europe and Japan, the United States
could encourage reductions in purchases of New Zealand lamb and
dairy products.[63]

Coinciding with the *Financial Times* report, United States Congressman
Dick Cheney (to become Secretary of Defense in 1989) introduced a Bill
that would bar imports from New Zealand and Australia.[64] According to
Cheney, he introduced the Bill because he was '[angered] by their
uncooperative attitude towards US international defence policy.... If
these countries are not willing to share the burden and responsibility of
defending freedom, why should we facilitate their enjoyment of freedom's
benefits such as unrestrained access to our markets....'[65] Although
Cheney's Bill (and others like it) was non-binding, it provided a forum at
committee hearings in Congress and the Senate for others to speak and
gave an indication of congressional attitudes towards New Zealand.

Within a day of Cheney's Bill, a resolution was introduced to the US
Senate by Republican William Cohen. The resolution was non-binding –
designed to 'persuade rather than force' – and sought to remove the
'injury test' on New Zealand's imports to the United States from 1 April
1985.[66] The 'injury test' is so called because American producers seeking
to have penal tariffs imposed on subsidised New Zealand imports must

63. All cited in ibid.
64. Cohen's Bill included Australia because at this time Bob Hawke had reneged on an
earlier commitment to provide support facilities in Australia for long-range tests of
America's MX missile.
65. Quoted in *The Press*, 11 February 1985.
66. Hugh Nevill, 'Trade Barrier Talks on the Agenda', *The Dominion*, 11 February 1985.

first prove that those imports are reducing their profits.[67]

Whilst denying that the American administration would impose any such economic sanctions on New Zealand, two (unnamed) officials announced that in the past New Zealand had benefited from administrative help to defeat 'protectionist' Bills. That support, based on the argument that New Zealand deserved special help as a loyal ally, would no longer apply they said.[68]

It should be remembered that Cheney's Bill and Cohen's resolution were introduced for the consumption of a New Zealand audience as much as the United States Congress or Senate. To an audience with little detailed knowledge of the intricacies of the US political system, any threat of trade bills – whether or not they had a chance of being passed – was bound to sow a few seeds of doubt in many people's minds about the wisdom of supporting the nuclear-free policies of the Labour-government.

The *National Business Review* in New Zealand acknowledged that formal sanctions were 'unthinkable', but nevertheless felt that the Reagan administration had left the way open for '[some] sort of behaviour which will not be helpful to New Zealand's trading interests.'[69]

David Lange, too, admitted for the first time that New Zealand would have to work harder in Washington if it were to stall protectionist moves aimed at New Zealand's exports in the wake of the nuclear ships ban: 'I have never said anything other that that we will have to work very hard to defeat those [protectionist] measures. . . . And if the administration is not disposed towards us . . . the task will be harder.'[70]

Whilst Lange was speaking, news of another possible trade reprisal was announced in the United States. The Under Secretary of State for Agriculture, Mr Daniel Amstutz, was reported to be considering a move to dump US surplus dairy products on the world market.[71] The 'dairy dumping' proposal was subsequently rejected by the Americans, but United States trade representative Bill Brock strongly suggested that the 'injury test' would be removed from New Zealand imports after 31 March.[72]

67. See Hugh Nevill, 'Senator Calls for Severe Punishment', *The Dominion*, 8 February 1985.
68. Ibid.
69. David Barber, 'The ANZUS Crunch: Now That Cost Has to be Counted', *National Business Review*, vol. 16, no. 4 (issue 610), 11 February 1985, p. 9.
70. Quoted in Richard Long, 'ANZUS Ban Means Hard Work Ahead', *The Dominion*, 15 February 1985.
71. Reported in *The Press*, 15 February 1985.
72. 'Americans Scrap Dairy Dumping Reprisal', *The Dominion*, 16 February 1985.

As was becoming the norm, all that New Zealand's Trade Minister Mike Moore could say was that his government accepted the assurance of the Reagan administration that no trade sanctions would be used to retaliate against New Zealand. By effectively reminding the United States of this 'promise' not to retaliate with trade sanctions, New Zealand was, in a small way, exerting its own pressure on the Reagan administration who at an official level were keen to avoid accusations of bullying New Zealand back into nuclear line.

As the dust began to settle after the furore of the *Buchanan* refusal, Congressional hearings on the state of New Zealand–United States relations were held in Washington. As a barometer of Congressional opinion on New Zealand's policies and the action (if any) that the United States should take, they were most revealing.

The Congressional Hearings

On 18 March the United States Congressional Sub-committee on East Asian and Pacific Affairs held hearings on the 'Security Treaty between Australia, New Zealand and the United States'.[73] During the day a long list of speakers – some members of the Committee, others invited guests – gave testimonies to the Committee regarding their perceptions of the ANZUS/nuclear ships dispute. Most (though not all) were critical of New Zealand's policy and suggested strategies the US should adopt in order to overturn the ships-ban. Perhaps above all else, it was strikingly apparent that the Congressional hearings provided a forum for a bi-partisan attack on New Zealand's policies from an ostensibly Democrat-controlled Congress.

Most witnesses at the hearings advised 'patience' with New Zealand; believing that given several months to reflect on the military 'costs' of the policy, the New Zealand government would realise the error of its ways and once again welcome American warships under the neither-confirm-nor-deny policy.

With this in mind, Guy Molinari (Republican, New York) strongly inferred that the US should go over the head of the New Zealand government and appeal directly to the New Zealand people:

73. *Security Treaty Between Australia, New Zealand and the United States*, Hearing before the Sub-committee on Asian and Pacific Affairs of the Committee on Foreign Affairs House of Representatives, 69th Congress, First Session, 18 March 1985. (US Government Printing Office, Washington 1985, 52–967–0.)

The congressional response at this time should foster support in New Zealand for a reversal. We should let some time pass to permit the full impact of its decision to be realised by New Zealand. . . . We should be appealing to the better instincts of the New Zealand people so that support grows for a reversal of the port access ban.[74]

If there was no tangible change in the New Zealand policy by the summer of 1985, Molinari argued that the US should adopt 'harsher measures', without specifying what these might be.

Congressman Toby Roth (Republican, Wisconsin) advocated a hard line on trade since New Zealand was a 'tremendous competitor' to US farmers, and he declared: 'I don't want to see us get kicked in the shins so that some politicians in New Zealand can grandstand.'[75] Henry Albinski (who, as we saw in Chapter 5, established an ANZUS 'think-tank' at the Georgetown University Center for Strategic and International Studies) claimed that New Zealanders were 'not much into seeing the world in terms of complex images',[76] and that applying pressure on them could 'translate into a nationalism that over time would be difficult to neutralise':[77] 'Perceived heavy pressure can have long-term counter-productive effects. It is an effect that could make it difficult for the National Party to resume office in 1987.'[78] Albinski concluded that the US was faced with 'unpalatable choices' in deciding what action it could take, and therefore perhaps should do nothing *overt* (our emphasis).[79] He did not suggest what covert actions, if any, the Reagan administration should undertake. In a similar vein, Congressman Stephen Solarz (Democrat, New York) argued that: 'there is no way the current government of New Zealand is going to be persuaded *on the merits of the issue* to change its policy. . . . We ought to be under no illusions that continuation of dialog is going to result in a change in the policy. It won't' (our emphasis).[80] Only by an ultimatum of 'no port calls – no ANZUS Treaty' would New Zealand be brought back into line according to Solarz and other speakers at the hearings.

However, some speakers were not so adamant that a negotiated settlement could not be reached. Professor William Tow of the University of Southern California, for example, urged the administration to 'negotiate

74. Ibid., p. 5.
75. Ibid., p. 17.
76. Ibid., p. 94.
77. Ibid.
78. Ibid.
79. Ibid., p. 96.
80. Ibid., pp. 134–5.

until hell freezes over'.[81]

A major concern which emerged during the Committee hearings was the possible 'ripple effect' of New Zealand's nuclear-free policies. Japan, Australia and the NATO countries were all mentioned as possible nations which could adopt similar nuclear-free policies to those in New Zealand, but arguably most important (in the sense also of being the most likely) was the Philippines with whom the US was in the process of re-negotiating its lease on military facilities in the country. Retired US Admiral Eugene Carroll (who spoke in support of New Zealand's policy) also warned the hearings that a similar policy in the Philippines would have 'extraordinarily negative consequences for the United States'.[82] Hence, as far as the US was concerned, the real issue at stake was not the ANZUS Treaty or port accessibility in New Zealand, but rather the prevention of the New Zealand 'nuclear allergy' spreading to more strategically 'significant' countries. In reading the transcripts of the Congressional hearings, it becomes obvious that this posed a great dilemma for the Reagan administration. If the real reason for the harsh reaction to New Zealand's nuclear warships ban was to prevent other 'allies' following suit, how could this be explained (let alone justified) to the New Zealand people. Punishing New Zealand might prevent other countries following the nuclear-free path, but it clearly would do very little to engender support for the United States in New Zealand.

Nevertheless, the rhetoric of the hearings continued along the increasingly familiar lines, with James Kelly, the Assistant Deputy General Secretary for East Asian and Pacific Affairs at the Department of Defense, maintaining that the US policy towards New Zealand continued to be '[the] restoration of unfettered port access without impinging on our policy of neither confirming nor denying the presence or absence of nuclear weapons on board our ships'.[83] A recurrent theme at the hearings was that New Zealand was perceived as wanting the benefits of an alliance with the United States without bearing any of the burdens (such as port calls by US warships).[84] And there was near unanimity by those speakers opposing the ships-ban that, after an appropriate 'cooling off period', if New Zealand still refused to admit US warships under the neither-

81. Ibid., p. 137.
82. Ibid., p. 139.
83. Ibid., p. 157.
84. See, for example, the testimony of Paul Wolfowitz at the Congressional Hearings (*Security Treaty Between Australia, New Zealand and the United States*, esp. p. 187).

confirm-nor-deny policy, then measures should be taken to end the ANZUS Treaty and pursue a bilateral defence policy with Australia.[85]

The overall tone of the Sub-committee hearings was cautious, but nevertheless adamant that New Zealand could not be permitted to get away with its nuclear-free policies without some cost – explicitly in the military sphere, and implicitly in the economic/trading area.

However, some speakers at the hearings did express either support for New Zealand, or at least a concern at the American response. For example, Anne Martindell, a former US Ambassador to New Zealand, said: 'I feel the US reaction to barring the ships was an over-reaction . . . . We don't want to be seeming to confront or provoke such a loyal ally. . . . Are we going to become a mirror image of our great enemy, and act as if our allies should be treated as satellites?'[86] And several others agreed that port access to New Zealand was not essential, that the ANZUS Treaty did not obligate the hosting of nuclear warships, and that under the provisions of the Treaty there was no absolute guarantee that the United States would come to the defence of New Zealand anyway.[87]

However, the 'anti-New Zealand' faction held the day. Their arguments were the ones that carried, and were given the widest coverage. In spite of the lengthy deliberations over possible further reprisals, the overall feeling appeared to be that New Zealand should be given time to 'think again' before the United States took any further (overt) actions. The proposed introduction of nuclear-free legislation by the Lange government (thus codifying the ships-ban in law) was also seen as being an indication of whether the government was going to, in the words of one speaker, act 'responsibly' or not.[88]

Just as there had been a six-month hiatus between the election of the Labour government and the USS *Buchanan* request, so it seemed that there would be another four to five month pause to allow New Zealand time to 'reflect' on its actions, and allow the diplomats on both sides to attempt to find a solution.

Nevertheless, the intention of the United States to spread the fear of trade reprisals among New Zealand exporters at this time was beginning

85. See, for example, the testimony of Stephen Solarz at the Congressional Hearings, ibid., esp. p. 187.
86. Ibid., p. 42.
87. See, for example, the testimonies of William Tow (ibid., p. 128), Anne Martindell (ibid., p. 128) and Eugene Carroll (ibid., p. 63), at the US Congressional Hearings.
88. Guy Molinari, ibid., p. 6.

to have the desired effect. For example, a Federated Farmers' spokesperson told an Auckland conference: 'The Government is naive in the extreme if it believes that trade will not suffer . . . I ask the Prime Minister to separate idealism from the cold hard facts of commercial reality.'[89] And the chairperson of the Meat Producers' Board in New Zealand, Adam Begg, after returning from a trip to the United States, was quick to draw a similar conclusion. He claimed that because of the nuclear ships ban life would become increasingly difficult for New Zealand exporters.[90]

It appeared as if almost every New Zealand exporter to North America began warning the government of the trade costs of the nuclear ships ban and some, like New Zealand Dairy Board Chairman Jim Graham, went so far as to demand compensation for lost exports: 'Our concern must be to ensure that when a moral stand has a financial cost, no Government economic measures are made which place and leave that cost on particular sectors of the community alone.'[91] Addressing a meeting of farmers, he said that the New Zealand Dairy Board was dropping promotions which used the words 'New Zealand' in the United States,[92] and several companies in New Zealand reported lost trade because of the ships-ban. The New Zealand Timber Federation, for example, received a letter from a furniture company in Virginia, USA, which concluded: 'Until your Government changes its policies concerning mutual co-operation with its former allies, I do not think this company would be interested in doing business with your country. . . .'[93] Another company, Monarch Trading, which sells sheepskins and fashion clothing via mail-order outlets in the US, also reported receiving letters critical of New Zealand's nuclear-free stance,[94] and a New Zealand ice cream was dropped by the Safeway supermarket chain in the US because of 'falling sales' which were attributed to the country of origin rather than the product itself.[95]

There were, in fact, few concrete examples of export losses, but the seeds of doubt had effectively been sown, and thus the perception was

89. Quoted in 'Trade Backlash Predicted', *The Dominion*, 21 February 1985.
90. Reported in Anne Byrnes, 'Meat Man Fears Trouble in US', *The Evening Post*, 28 February 1985.
91. Quoted in 'Call to Spread Cost of Nuclear Stand', *The Dominion*, 5 March 1985.
92. Cited in David Barber, 'US Nuclear Storm Clouds Brewing on the Traders' Horizons', *National Business Review*, vol. 16, no. 8 (issue 614), 11 March 1985, p. 12.
93. Quoted in 'US Company Cuts Off Million-Dollar Business', *The Dominion*, 7 March 1985.
94. Cited in Barber, 'US Nuclear Storm Clouds', p. 12.
95. Ibid.

created that any lost orders, or increase in red tape, etc., was due entirely to the 'economic cost' of the ships-ban.

February – March 1985: The Media Reaction

Not only did the Lange government have to contend with the military, and threatened trade, reprisals, they also had to face a largely hostile media.

As we have already seen, the Reagan administration reacted angrily to the denial of access to New Zealand ports. This anger was matched in the media, and a proliferation of editorials after the USS *Buchanan* was denied port facilities unleashed a stream of invective against Lange and his government's policies.

One particularly vitriolic editorial appeared in the *New York Tribune*. Under the heading 'Behind New Zealand's Bad Mouth', it said: 'We hope the Socialist bums ensconced in Wellington will get thrown out as they predictably botch both the domestic and foreign policy of a great nation.'[96] In similar vein, *The Nation* called New Zealand an 'enemy within' because of its 'nuclear allergy'.[97] Other US editorials attacked New Zealanders as 'mutton headed', 'ostriches', 'Soviet stooges', 'freeloaders' and 'isolationists'.[98] The *Baltimore Sun* called New Zealanders 'sanctimonious antipodians',[99] and the *Washington Post* wondered if there was 'something in the water Down Under'.[100]

In Britain, the media reaction was much the same. The *Economist* decided that even though everyone liked the 'nice' New Zealand people, they really couldn't be allowed to eat their ANZUS cake and 'spit out the rather tiny nuclear currant'.[101] In a lengthy editorial it was made clear that New Zealand's action was the height of irresponsibility – 'attempting to assert nuclear innocence in a nuclear world'.[102] As was the norm in most

---

96. Cited in Hugh Nevill, 'US Rumbles Continue Over N-Ship Warning', *The Press*, 19 February 1985.
97. 'Nuclear Allergy', *The Nation*, vol. 240, no. 7, 23 February 1985.
98. Cited in Andrew Mack, 'Crisis in the Other Alliance: ANZUS in the 1980s', *World Policy Journal* (New York), vol. 13, no. 3, summer 1986, pp. 447–72.
99. Cited in Jason Salzman, 'NZ Nuclear Reality', *Peacelink* (NZ), February 1987, p. 4.
100. 'Nuclear Allergy', *Washington Post*, 8 February 1985. (Cited in USIA Wireless File F–16 EP519, 8 February 1985.)
101. 'The Kiwi Innocent – New Zealand has to Help Itself to be Protected', *The Economist*, 2 March 1985, p. 12.
102. Ibid.

editorials of this nature, New Zealand's action was seen as a 'gesture', and a self-damaging one at that.

New Zealand's geographical isolation was interpreted as a reason for their obvious innocence in nuclear matters, as an article in the *Baltimore Sun* made clear: 'New Zealand is a small country a long way from the continental United States, and its views of the world don't travel very far from that area.'[103]

Not all the foreign media were opposed to New Zealand's ban on nuclear warships. The *Tribune* newspaper of Oakland, California, suggested that New Zealand will have done the United States a favour if '[its] act of independence makes Americans pause and consider whether the United States really needs nuclear weapons for forward power projection . . .'[104] And the left-wing *New York Guardian* implored New Zealand to 'stand firm' and argued that the ANZUS Treaty was an aggressive alliance aimed against independence movements in the Pacific or any 'weakening of Western control'.[105]

In Britain, the *New Statesman* and the *Guardian* were virtually alone in supporting New Zealand. In an editorial, the *New Statesman* said that David Lange had 'broken the depressing pattern of socialist politicians who say one thing about defence in opposition but openly or secretly go back on it all in office'.[106]

The New Zealand media were caught in something of a dilemma. There was no way that they supported the ships-ban and nuclear-free policies, but there was a grudging respect for the fact that the Labour Party had carried out its pledges in the face of growing pressure from the United States in particular, but also Australia and Britain. However, there were also the customary outright condemnations of the policies, one of which was published in the Christchurch-based *Press* newspaper in early March:

> The Government has made foolish decisions based on a foolish policy. . . . The decision to ban the warships . . . is probably the most monumental blunder of the post-war years. If New Zealand decides not to behave as a responsible member of the Western system of alliances, it

103. J.G.A. Pocock, 'Behind the Crisis, New Zealand and the United States', *Baltimore Sun*, 12 February 1985. (Cited in USIA Wireless file EP201 M24–024 12 February 1985.)
104. 'Toward a pacific South Pacific', *The Tribune* (Oakland, California), 12 February 1985, p. B–6.
105. 'Stand Firm Kiwi's (Guardian Viewpoint), *The Guardian* (New York), 20 February 1985.
106. 'New Zealand Stands Up to be Counted', *New Statesman* (London), vol. 109, no. 2812, 8 February 1985, pp. 2–3.

cannot expect to continue receiving the very wide range of benefits that its loyalty, until recent weeks, has ensured.[107]

We have seen already that the Labour government was facing opposition to its nuclear ships ban on all fronts. There were the military reprisals, the threatened trade sanctions, and the widespread hostility from the media. In New Zealand, too, the government was facing up to criticism from the National Party Opposition, and there were indications of a grassroots campaign to undermine the ships-ban. It is this 'domestic' reaction that we now examine.

February – March 1985: The 'Domestic' Pressures

On 12 February, the New Zealand Parliament re-convened after the summer recess, and was immediately plunged into an adjournment debate on New Zealand–United States relations.

The then leader of the Opposition, Jim McLay, moved the adjournment and launched a bitter attack on Labour's nuclear ships ban. The debate occurred in the wake of the military reprisals and thinly-veiled threats of trade sanctions that the United States had imposed on New Zealand, and in the midst of the ensuing debate over the nuclear/non-nuclear nature of the ANZUS Treaty.

According to McLay, the downgrading of military intelligence from the United States and the cancellation of exercises such as *Sea Eagle* were the thin end of a wedge which effectively ended the ANZUS alliance. In Parliament he claimed that the nuclear-free policies of the government did not even make sense. Specifically on the ships-ban he said:

> It is a policy that claims to act in the cause of nuclear disarmament, but the Prime Minister knows full well it does nothing to advance the cause of nuclear disarmament. . . . It does not make New Zealand any safer, it does not make the South Pacific any safer, and it does not make the world any safer. . . . Banning the ships from a New Zealand port does nothing for the cause of nuclear disarmament, but it does enormous damage to New Zealand's defence interests.[108]

107. 'A Future in Sandcastle NZ', *The Press*, 6 March 1985.
108. *Parliamentary Debates (Hansard)*, 1st Session, 41st Parliament 1984–5, House of Representatives, vol. 460, p. 2896.

The National Party Opposition essentially used two main arguments in the debate. Firstly, McLay and his colleagues repeatedly asserted that the National Party was the true 'nuclear disarmament party' – in that they were committed to supporting disarmament, an end to nuclear testing and so on. Secondly, they continually claimed that the Labour policies would destroy the ANZUS alliance.

On the first argument, whatever the National Party may have claimed to be had not been backed up by much action when they formed the government. It is true to say that they opposed nuclear testing in the Pacific but this opposition had been stronger on rhetoric than action. And on the visit of nuclear warships to New Zealand ports, it is perhaps sufficient to say that if the National Party had been the party of government, then these warship visits would have continued.

On the second argument, the issues are perhaps more involved. The National Party clearly believed that the possible collapse of ANZUS was the weak link in Labour's policies. Public opinion polls at the time certainly indicated that whilst a majority of people supported the ban on nuclear ships (about 60 to 70 per cent), roughly an equal percentage wanted New Zealand to remain in ANZUS. A simple enough argument on the surface, but as the peace movement in New Zealand pointed out, it is far from certain whether the full implications of ANZUS membership were commonly known. Rather, it was suggested that ANZUS tends to be a 'buzz' word, evoking positive feelings of 'security', 'stability', 'freedom' and the like, in the minds of many New Zealanders.[109] (This could easily be transposed to Britain using NATO instead of ANZUS.) This argument was supported by the results of a questionnaire carried out for the 1986 Defence Committee of Enquiry, which showed seemingly contradictory answers to slightly differently worded questions on whether or not to remain in a security alliance.[110]

During the parliamentary debate on 12 February, the National Party spokespeople consistently played the 'ANZUS is destroyed' card. In response Labour speakers maintained that ANZUS was not at the point of destruction, but that there needed to be an acceptance by the United States and Australia that it was never meant to be a *nuclear* alliance. As one commentator has noted, this claim by the Labour government that

109. See, for example, Elsie Locke and John Gallagher, 'Defence and Security', *New Zealand Monthly Review*, vol. XXVII no. 293–4, November/December 1986, pp. 9–11.
110. 'Defence and Security: What New Zealanders Want', Report of the Defence Committee of Enquiry, July 1986. Government Printer, Wellington, pp. 40–1.

the treaty possessed no nuclear operational component, and their reassurance that the pact would remain in force, 'met with the American contradiction it invited'.[111]

To many onlookers from overseas (both proponents and opponents of the ships-ban), it appeared that the Labour government was embarked on a radical course of action which challenged the very core of American global military strategy. In fact, apart from the disagreement over the nuclear ships issue, the government was at pains to stress that it did not question America's role and strategy in the Pacific, or indeed elsewhere around the globe. In the words of David Lange:

> However much we may disagree at times, an underlying affinity between New Zealand and the United States surpasses all our differences. . . . The United States has been forthright and straightforward. It has told us its position, and we have told it ours. We can work that through, and we will work it through because the United States understands . . . that there is more to our relationship than nuclear weapons.[112]

However, it was all rather one-sided – there was little of the same kind of conciliatory message coming back from the United States. It was also during the parliamentary debate on 12 February that a further contradiction on the Labour side was highlighted. A succession of Labour speakers emphasised the international aspect of the ships-ban. Deputy Prime Minister Geoffrey Palmer called it a policy which 'will provide hope for the world'.[113] Education Minister Russell Marshall called the ban 'an act of tremendous political courage',[114] and there was talk of New Zealand's policy being a 'beacon of hope' for the world, and an inspiration to peace movements everywhere (which it undoubtedly was). The contradiction among all this euphoria was that on several occasions the Prime Minister had vigorously denied that New Zealand was in any way setting an example for others to follow. 'Our policy is not for export' was an oft-repeated remark used by David Lange, whilst at the same time many of his MPs were enthusing about the global impact of the ships-ban.

Despite the criticism of Labour's nuclear-free policies from the

---

111. Alan Robson, 'New Zealand's Anti-Nuclear Cold War', *School of Social and Economic Development Working Paper No 3*, The University of the South Pacific, Suva, Fiji, June 1986, p. 5.
112. *Parliamentary Debates*, 1984–5, p. 2900
113. Ibid., p. 2906.
114. Ibid., p. 2911.

National Party Opposition, and the sometimes less than unified approach to the international ramifications of the policy from government members, the ships-ban remained, and Labour stood firm. Geoffrey Palmer summed up the government's determination to see the policy through when he said: 'The Opposition want New Zealanders to cower, to give in, to follow policies that are dictated by others. The Government will not buckle to those pressures and its policy will be followed unrelentingly.'[115]

Outside of the parliamentary debating chamber, the domestic pressures for the government to rescind the ships-ban began in earnest. For example, the Chairman of the Canterbury Chamber of Commerce, Mr Martin Jolly, urged that the government having 'had the centre-stage of the world theatre to express its opposition to nuclear arms', should return to the nuclear fold as a Western ally, and thus save New Zealand's economy from an angry Congress and Senate.[116]

An immediate reaction to the cancelling of the *Sea Eagle* exercise was sought from, and given by, several retired or former New Zealand defence staff. The former chief of New Zealand's Army staff, Major-General Robin Williams, declared that: 'New Zealand cannot gain from the Government's actions . . . there will be cause for great regret in the future.'[117] Likewise, former Chief of Defence Staff, Sir Richard Bolt, said that New Zealand's ability to 'influence and pressure' for a reduction in nuclear arms would be 'reduced, not enhanced by the Government's actions'.[118] This was not to be the only time that former military officers were to publicly announce their disquiet at the government's defence and foreign policies.

It was in February, too, that the first of a number of pro-ANZUS pressure groups was set up in New Zealand. Dr Jim Sprott, an Auckland scientist, had been vocal in his opposition to Labour's nuclear-free policies since before the 1984 election. He accused Labour of weakening the nuclear deterrent, and he was forthright in his support for the Reagan administration's nuclear-war-fighting policies.[119] Dr Sprott's pressure group was called 'Peace Through Security' and thus bore a remarkably similar name to the American 'Coalition for Peace Through Strength',

115. Ibid., p. 2906.
116. 'NZ Should Line Up with the United States', *The Press*, 27 February 1985.
117. Quoted in Paul Sheehan, 'NZ Feels Fall-out of Anti-Nuclear Stand', *Sydney Morning Herald*, 6 February 1985.
118. Ibid.
119. See Dennis Small, 'Pro-Nuclear Backlash. The Strange Case of Dr. Sprott', *New Zealand Review*, vol. XXVII, no. 275, April 1985, pp. 3–4.

and the British 'Coalition for Peace Through Security'. His group's arguments also echoed those of the American and British groups – claiming among other things that the peace movement in New Zealand was infiltrated by communists and manipulated from Moscow.[120]

Perhaps surprisingly, the 'Peace Through Security' group was the only such organisation to emerge at this time. It was not until the latter part of 1985 and early 1986 that several other pro-nuclear/ANZUS groups were established.

The months of February and March 1985 saw a period of intense activity and pressure on the Labour government to compromise or abandon the nuclear ships ban. As we have seen, military reprisals, warnings and threats were the order of the day, and the ban on nuclear ships was trivialised and ridiculed in an attempt to embarrass the Labour leadership. In the following chapter the main events of April 1985 to December 1986 will be described, as more reprisals and threats to New Zealand's nuclear-free policies became apparent.

120. See Dennis Small, 'The Rise of the Pro-Nuclear Right', *New Zealand Monthly Review*, vol. XXVII, no. 293–4, November – December 1986, pp. 5–8.

CHAPTER 8

Pressures Sustained:
April 1985 – December 1986

As the dust settled on the immediate reactions to the *Buchanan* affair, the longer-term attempts to undermine and overturn the ships-ban began to unfold. The pressures on New Zealand to rescind the ban were to continue throughout the year and into 1986, but there was not the intensity of the actions/reactions of the first two months. Indeed, many of the later events of 1985/6 echoed and repeated those of February and March. There were, for example, many more thinly-veiled threats of trade sanctions; but even if the messenger varied, the message remained essentially the same. Likewise with media editorials, and to a degree also with the 'official' pronouncements from Washington. To spend time detailing each new trade warning, each press editorial and each expression of anger from Washington, Canberra or London would be rather like playing the same record over and over again – at different speeds and volume perhaps, but the same record nevertheless.

Hence, this chapter will tend to summarise where the previous two have detailed, and concentrate instead on the new developments in the dispute which arose during the remainder of 1985 and throughout 1986. To begin with, it will be useful to look at a few of the more significant trade-related pressures and predictions.

Trade

One interesting aspect of the warnings over the 'trade costs' of the nuclear-free policies was that these warnings were not borne out by the facts. For example, several New Zealand companies began to see the ANZUS row as attracting American tourists in greater numbers to New Zealand. Mount Cook Airlines reported their busiest summer season with tourists from the United States,[1] and a trade mission visiting New Zealand from the Seattle-based Puget Sound Chamber of Commerce categorically denied suggestions that the ships-ban was having any effect on consumer attitudes to New Zealand in the US.[2] By the beginning of May 1985 the New Zealand Manufacturers' Federation reported that it had still received no reports from member manufacturers of orders lost as a result of the Lange government's anti-nuclear stance.[3] And, as if to prove the point conclusively, Wattie Industries reported that their creme caramel and chocolate puddings were being consumed at a rate of 400 a day in, of all places, the Pentagon.[4]

This is not to imply that there were not real fears that exports with North America would suffer because of the ships-ban, but what was happening was that a protectionist lobby in Congress was using the ships-ban as an *additional* reason for imposing some form of restrictions on New Zealand imports. It is worth remembering that up to 300 different bills with protectionist elements were before Congress at this time.[5] Calls for a reduction in New Zealand Casein imports, for example, would have been made anyway, although there is some merit in the argument that such calls may have received a wider and more sympathetic hearing because of the ANZUS dispute.

In late October, nineteen New Zealand business leaders returned from a trade mission to the United States and urged the Labour government to 'de-escalate' the row over the nuclear ships ban. Reporting on the reaction the mission received in Washington, spokesperson Sir Alan Hellaby said: 'It is a very political issue. . . . We have put it exactly as it has been put to us. Therefore it is quite clear to us that unless we can get a de-escalation, we are going to find it more difficult to get a good trading relationship with

1. 'ANZUS Row Possible Drawback', *The Evening Post*, 6 April 1985.
2. 'US Consumers Unmoved by ANZUS Disagreement', *The Dominion*, 15 April 1985.
3. 'US Orders', *Manufacturer* (Journal of the NZ Manufacturers Federation), 6 May 1985.
4. 'Proof of the Pudding', *The Press*, 29 May 1985.
5. Cited in David Barber, 'Pro-protectionist Pressure Running High in US', *National Business Review*, 26 August 1985.

the United States Government. . . ."[6]

The timing of this statement, however, could hardly have been more inappropriate. On the following day the new Department of Trade and Industry figures were released which showed that in the year ending June 1985 the value of exports to America increased by 49.1 per cent to nearly $NZ1.6 billion.[7] According to Trade and Industry trade services director Peter Finkle, the figures showed that it was not all 'gloom and doom' on the American market despite the ANZUS row.[8] But the year ended on a familiar note, with both the US Embassy Commercial Attache and Economic Counsellor warning that, unlike many times before, the US administration would not be so inclined to go in and 'bat' on New Zealand's behalf when Congress was demanding protectionist measures against New Zealand imports.[9]

Aside from the continued rumblings on trade matters, 1985 also saw the first signs of possible British involvement in the dispute. In early March, the British Minister for Defence Procurement, Adam Butler, ruled out any possibility of Britain adopting a mediatory role in the ANZUS row,[10] and in early May – responding to rumours of a higher British profile in the dispute – a British government official said that there would be no requests for port calls to New Zealand by vessels of the Royal Navy, although speculation continued to mount that the Royal Navy might agree to exercise with Australian and New Zealand forces in October 1986.[11]

It was reported in September, however, that John Stanley, the British Minister for the Armed Forces, had made it very clear at a meeting in Wellington with David Lange that Britain would not compromise on its own policy of neither-confirming-nor-denying the presence of nuclear weapons on board its warships, and therefore Britain would not be seeking port facilities in New Zealand.[12] Overall, however, the impression was given that Whitehall – despite its distaste for the nuclear ships ban –

---

6. Quoted in Richard Long, 'Lange, Business Differ on ANZUS', *The Dominion*, 29 October 1985.
7. Cited in Andrew Pirie, 'Trade Booms Despite Nuke Row', *The Dominion*, 30 October 1985.
8. Ibid.
9. See, for example, 'Is America Going to Block our Exports?' (Professional Briefing), *The Accountants' Journal* (NZ), vol. 64, no. 11, December 1985, pp. 6–7.
10. 'Mediator Role for Britain Rejected', *The Dominion*, 1 March 1985.
11. 'UK Might Side-Step N-ship Port Clash', *The Press*, 7 May 1985.
12. Frank Cranston, 'RN Deployment May Exclude New Zealand', *Jane's Defence Weekly*, 28 September 1985, p. 677.

did not want to increase the 'diplomatic problems' that New Zealand was facing over its defence differences with Washington.[13]

The Bombing of the *Rainbow Warrior*

If the British were still keeping a relatively low profile in the dispute, the same could not be said of the French who indirectly, and certainly unintentionally, were to harden anti-nuclear feelings in New Zealand. The flagship of the environmentalist pressure group Greenpeace, the *Rainbow Warrior*, had docked at Auckland harbour on 7 July to prepare for a sailing to the French nuclear testing site at Mururoa Atoll. On 10 July the ship was sunk by two limpet mines. One of the crew members of the *Warrior*, Fernando Pereira, was killed in the bombing.

The bombing led to the most extensive investigation ever undertaken by the police in New Zealand. The arrest of two French citizens travelling on false Swiss passports immediately aroused suspicion that the French government might have been involved in the bombing, but this was repeatedly denied by the Mitterand administration for almost a month. Amid growing speculation of direct French involvement, President Mitterrand promised to investigate fully the accusations that the French secret service were behind the bombing. Mitterrand also promised that those responsible would be brought to justice irrespective of their position in France. On 25 August a twenty-nine page report was delivered to the French government by Bernard Tricot, a senior French civil servant who had been mandated to conduct a thorough enquiry into the bombing. The report confirmed that the French security agency, the Direction générale de la sécurité extérieure (DGSE), had been keeping the Greenpeace nuclear protests under surveillance in the Pacific, and that there were plans to infiltrate future Greenpeace sailings to Moruroa Atol. The two French citizens, Dominique Prieur and Alain Mafart, who had been arrested in New Zealand were admitted to be agents of the DGSE, but Tricot's report claimed that there was no evidence that they, or any other French agents, had planted the bombs which sunk the *Rainbow Warrior*.

However, the fact that the DGSE were involved in infiltrating the Greenpeace organisation, and had agents in New Zealand led to the French Defence Minister Charles Hernu resigning his post on 20 September,

13. 'UK Might Side-Step N-ship Port Clash'.

quickly followed by Admiral Pierre Lacoste, the head of the French foreign intelligence service. On 22 September the French Prime Minister Laurent Fabius finally admitted that 'agents of the DGSE sank this boat. They acted on orders.'[14]

In New Zealand, Prieur and Marfart were sentenced to ten years imprisonment on charges of manslaughter. The French reaction was not one of humility, but rather one of outrage that their two agents – acting under orders – would have to serve their sentences in New Zealand and not France. In an effort to have their agents returned home, the French government began to apply economic sanctions against New Zealand exports. The importation of sheep's brains, meat, fish, kiwi fruit and wool was blocked or impeded, and warning noises were made regarding the amount of imports to Europe of New Zealand butter. David Lange's response was to deny categorically that there was any possibility of the agents returning to France and freedom. Nevertheless, the economic leverage being used by France ensured that by 19 June 1986 the United Nations Secretary-General Javier Perez de Cuellar was to become a third-party mediator in the dispute. After lengthy negotiations, a decision was reached whereby in return for compensation of US$7m and a formal apology from France, the two agents would be transferred to the French Polynesian island of Hao for three years to continue their sentences. It was an agreement which led to much criticism of David Lange in New Zealand, particularly given his previous unconditional assurances that the two agents would not be released from New Zealand. In reality, however, he was given very little choice considering the powerful economic leverage which France was able to use, especially within the EEC.

The material since written on the *Rainbow Warrior* bombing and the subsequent capture and imprisonment of two of its perpetrators is voluminous.[15] What is of great importance, however, is the reaction of New Zealanders to the bombing, and, perhaps more strikingly, the (non) reaction of the British and American governments.

In New Zealand, right across the political spectrum, there was an outrage against a country which, because of its nuclear testing programme in the Pacific and its colonial rule of New Caledonia (Kanaky), was not close to the hearts of most New Zealanders anyway. The net

14. Quoted in Ramesh Thakur, 'A Dispute of Many Colours: France, New Zealand and the "Rainbow Warrior" Affair', *The World Today*, December 1986, p. 210.
15. See, for example, Michael King, *Death of the Rainbow Warrior*, Penguin Books, London and New York, 1986.

result of the bombing was that it reinforced and hardened anti-nuclear attitudes and instilled a nationalistic pride and determination to maintain the nuclear-free policies. Additionally it increased awareness of, and opposition to, most things French in the South Pacific.

But the *Rainbow Warrior* sinking was also revealing in the context of New Zealand's relations with the United States and Britain. Whilst other leaders around the world condemned the bombing, the silence on the issue from Margaret Thatcher and Ronald Reagan was deafening. Both leaders refused to condemn the bombing outright – an American official even going to great lengths to defend the 'right' of France to test its nuclear weapons in the Pacific.[16] And when asked at the Tokyo economic summit of 1986 whether there was some hypocrisy in that summit (which included France) condemning state-sponsored terrorism in the light of the French action in New Zealand, British Prime Minister Margaret Thatcher responded: 'The two are totally different. Anyone who confuses them. . . . there is no point in wasting time on that question.'[17]

In a book on the nuclear ships ban in New Zealand, Stuart McMillan suggests that had Britain and the US not been in dispute with New Zealand at the time, they would have been vocal in condemning the French action.[18] If he is right, then such silence irrefutably illustrated the shallowness of the frequent British and American tirades against 'state terrorism'. The French sinking of a ship docked in the harbour of a friendly country was clearly an embarrassment to Thatcher, Reagan and their supporters, and their refusal unreservedly to deplore the bombing was quite properly interpreted by many New Zealanders as being equivalent to condoning the French sabotage.

Nuclear-Free Legislation

Amidst the fury surrounding the sinking of the *Rainbow Warrior*, the efforts at finding a solution to the impasse over the nuclear ships ban/ANZUS dispute continued. With the introduction of nuclear-free legislation due before Parliament by the end of the year (which would codify in law the nuclear ships ban), a new attempt was made by the Labour government

16. Quoted in Tom Bridgman, 'Nuclear-Free Declaration "Not Needed"', *The Evening Post*, 4 September 1985.
17. Quoted in Thakur, 'A Dispute of Many Colours', p. 216.
18. Stuart McMillan, *Neither Confirm Nor Deny – The nuclear ships dispute between New Zealand and the United States*, Allen & Unwin/Port Nicholson Press, Wellington, 1987, p. 140.

to find a compromise with the United States which would allow port calls to continue.

In fact, this 'new' attempt at finding a solution was not very new at all. It amounted to the onus of determining whether a ship or submarine violated the nuclear ban resting with the New Zealand Prime Minister, thus obviating the need for any US (or British) clarification. In essence, this was no different from when the USS *Buchanan* was refused entry. The United States refused to confirm or deny whether the ship would be carrying nuclear weapons, so Lange took the decision to bar the ship when he concluded that he could not be certain that it would not be carrying nuclear weapons. In September, Deputy Prime Minister Geoffrey Palmer visited Washington with the 'new' offer and, not surprisingly, US intransigence meant that he returned to New Zealand empty-handed. However, Palmer's visit was something of a diplomatic victory for the government. As Tony Garnier reported in the Wellington-based *Evening Post*: 'By sending Mr Palmer to Washington, the Government is obviously doing everything possible to keep the [ANZUS] treaty intact and blunt any American backlash. . . . Even if the strategy fails to break the impasse. . . . the Government will at least be able to publicly portray itself as having tried its utmost.'[19]

Palmer also took with him to Washington a draft copy of the nuclear-free legislation for the Americans to muse over and make any suggestions whereby the legislation and the US neither-confirm-nor-deny policy could be made compatible. News that Palmer had taken a copy of the proposed legislation for American 'approval' (and a copy was also sent to Britain) was met with fierce criticism in the New Zealand peace movement and sections of the Labour Party. It was feared that Lange was bowing to US pressure, and poised to make the legislation so ambiguous as to be almost useless. To this end, it was reported that the government had dropped provisions for a judicial review of any decision by a New Zealand Prime Minister which allowed a warship to visit.[20]

However, the US State Department was not impressed with Palmer's visit, and claimed that far from bringing concessions with him to Washington, he had in fact outlined the New Zealand position on a 'take-it-or-leave-it' basis.[21] By 27 September the US tone had reverted to

19. Tony Garnier, 'ANZUS Row Mark II', *The Evening Post*, 4 September 1985.
20. Nayan Chanda, 'Waiving the ANZUS Rules – Lange's Compromise has not Impressed the US Navy', *Far Eastern Economic Review*, 3 October 1985, pp. 36–7.
21. 'Palmer Quest Fails, But Talks Will Continue', *The Evening Post*, 23 September 1985.

its customary belligerency when State Department spokesman Bernard Kalb accused New Zealand of not attempting to resolve the issue (of banning nuclear ships), adding: 'Should removal of the port ban not be possible, and should New Zealand enact adverse legislation, we will have to revise New Zealand's continued status as a United States ally under ANZUS.'[22]

The *National Business Review* had dubbed Palmer's visit to Washington a 'do-or-die mission', and suggested that the government was undertaking a big gamble on the success of the trip, in the sense that it would be difficult to mount another mission without significant concessions which it was pledged not to make.[23] Their analysis was correct, and when Palmer returned to Wellington with no agreement, and no prospect of one, it was obvious that relations with the US would deteriorate further when the nuclear-free legislation was tabled before Parliament.

The New Zealand Nuclear Free Zone Disarmament and Arms Control Bill

In June 1985 David Lange previewed the draft nuclear-free New Zealand legislation before passing it on to his cabinet for approval. The *National Business Review* predicted that the United States would step up diplomatic activity in an attempt to stop the government introducing the legislation,[24] and it was probably no coincidence that Secretary of State George Shultz chose to use a speech to the East–West Centre at the University of Hawaii on 17 July to accuse New Zealand of 'walking off the job' of defending freedom.[25]

By October, however, the draft legislation was approved by the cabinet and Lange expressed anger at the refusal of the United States to discuss its wording. The legislation had, it seems, been further amended to appease the US and Britain, but neither country would enter into discussions with New Zealand over it. This refusal prompted Lange to comment: 'The spirit of Geneva lasted about 24 hours when it came to an ally. . . I hope

22. 'State Dept Threat to "Revise" NZ Ally Status', *The Evening Post*, 28 September 1985.
23. David Barber, 'Palmer on His Way in Do-or-Die Washington Mission', *National Business Review*, vol. 16, no. 34 (Issue 641), 16 September 1985, p. 16.
24. David Barber, 'No-compromise Foreign Policy Dominated by ANZUS', *National Business Review*, vol. 17, no. 25 (Issue 632), 15 July 1985, pp. 31–2.
25. Quoted in Shirley Christian, 'Shultz in Honolulu, Denounces New Zealand', *New York Times*, 18 July 1985.

it lasts longer with their friends in Russia.'[26] It was a hitherto unprecedented attack on the United States by Lange, and clearly illustrated his exasperation with the Reagan administration. He continued:

[The] Washington reaction might stamp out of me my affection for a country which believes in democratic principles and the principles of political accountability, and does not rely on sheer clout to exert from a small nation whatever it wants . . . I hope it will be a long time before I am reduced to that scepticism, but this sort of conduct drives me toward it . . . . [27]

On 10 December, the New Zealand Nuclear Free Zone Disarmament and Arms Control Bill was introduced to Parliament for the first time and passed its first reading on a 48–30 vote. The National Party Opposition claimed the bill would 'destroy ANZUS',[28] whilst the Labour government continued to maintain that the Bill was 'wholly compatible with New Zealand's international obligations', including those assumed under ANZUS.[29] The Coalition Against Nuclear Warships (CANWAR) called the legislation 'one of the important events in the worldwide efforts to free the world from the threat of nuclear weapons'.[30] The American reaction was hardly unexpected, with various officials predicting that Washington would almost certainly cut New Zealand out of ANZUS if Wellington enacted into law the policy of banning nuclear ships.

Worldnet 'Interactives'

In addition to the official statements from Washington, there were several other ways in which the United States was attempting to undermine popular support in New Zealand for the ships-ban, one of which was promoted by the USIA in October.

Worldnet 'interactives' are the means by which foreign journalists in up to five countries are able to interview US officials via a televised satellite link-up with Washington. The propaganda potential of this was first realised after the US invasion of Grenada, and since then the broadcasts

26. Quoted in 'PM Lashes US Refusal to Talk', *The Evening Post*, 26 November 1985.
27. Quoted in Richard Long, 'Nuke Ship Ban Passes Cabinet', *The Dominion*, 26 November 1985.
28. Richard Long, 'Ship Bill Allows Nukes Off Coastline', *The Dominion*, 11 December 1985.
29. Ibid.
30. Quoted in 'Nuke Bill Finally a Fizzer', *New Zealand Sunday Times*, 15 December 1985.

have become a major part of United States 'public diplomacy'.[31]

During 1985 two Worldnet broadcasts were shown on New Zealand television. The first, in October, featured US Secretary of Defense Caspar Weinberger who used the opportunity to decry the efforts of New Zealand to resolve the ANZUS row as 'patently unworkable. . . . and think that is the very kindest way to phrase it'.[32] His comments brought a furious reaction from New Zealand Deputy Prime Minister Geoffrey Palmer who (for the second time in as many months) accused the Americans of 'going over the head of the New Zealand Government' to influence public opinion.[33] Weinberger's interview was organised by the USIA, and was the first occasion in which Television New Zealand (TVNZ) had participated in such a link. The costs of the transmission from the United States were defrayed to a considerable extent by the USIA, causing controversy over the obvious political implications of a government agency subsidised transmission. In a response to the attack on Weinberger by Palmer, the United States Embassy in Wellington issued a press release defending Worldnet, Weinberger's participation in it, and TVNZ's decision to broadcast it.[34] At this time press statements on contentious issues from the US Embassy were extremely rare, but they were to appear with increasing regularity in 1986.

The second Worldnet interview was with the Secretary for East Asia and Pacific Affairs, Paul Wolfowitz, in December. Wolfowitz warned that if New Zealand enacted its anti-nuclear legislation the US would 'review' its defence co-operation with the country.[35] It is hard to believe that the timing of the broadcast and Wolfowitz's comments had nothing to do with the imminent tabling of the nuclear-free legislation in Parliament.

At the time of the Weinberger and Wolfowitz interviews, the then head of the New Zealand Broadcasting Corporation, Hugh Rennie, defended the decision to show them. But a new head of current affairs on TVNZ, John Scully, who took over soon after the Wolfowitz interview, imposed a virtual ban on TVNZ's participation in future Worldnet broadcasts,

31. See, for example, Murray McLaughlin, 'The Campaign to set New Zealand Thinking the USA Way', *New Zealand Sunday Times*, 30 November 1986.
32. Quoted in 'Weinberger's ANZUS Doctrine . . . ', *Pacific Islands Monthly*, December 1985, p. 19.
33. Quoted in Murray McLaughlin, 'Palmer Criticises US Nuke Ploy', *The Dominion*, 18 October 1985.
34. 'Statement Regarding the 16 October "East Asia Net" Broadcast Interview With American Secretary of Defense Weinberger', press release: United States Information Service, American Embassy, Wellington, 18 October 1985.
35. Cited in Karen Brown, 'US Not Saying How It Might do Things', *The Evening Post*, 5 December 1985.

saying: 'Why are they [the Americans] doing it? The answer's pretty simple . . . I've decided to treat Worldnet with the utmost caution.'[36]

In addition to the Worldnet broadcasts, the USIA in New Zealand was (and still is) active on a number of other fronts. In particular there are the International Visitor Programs (IVP) and American Participant (AM-PART) Programs in which 'influential' New Zealanders are sent on all-expenses paid visits to the United States, and important Americans are sent to New Zealand on speaking tours, etc. It has also been alleged that the USIA has frequently commissioned public opinion polls in New Zealand on the ships-ban/ANZUS issue, with the Heylen public opinion organisation. However, the USIA has consistently denied that this is the case. It will be worthwhile to spend some time now outlining these other activities of the USIA in New Zealand.

In 1986, under the Freedom of Information Act (FOIA) in America, information concerning the activities of the USIA in New Zealand was released to peace movement activists. Under the Reagan administration the USIA had its worldwide annual budget increased to over one billion US dollars, and was frequently criticised as being little more than a propagandist mouthpiece for the American right wing. The documents released showed that the USIA had a large team of officials in New Zealand (three Americans and twelve locals) in 1985–6. This was as many as the information sections of the Japanese (6), Soviet(4), British(2), French(2), and Australian(1) diplomatic posts put together.[37]

The International Visitor Program (IVP)

The information released under the FOIA showed that between 1983 and 1985 the USIA sent a total of 115 New Zealanders on fully paid trips to the United States at an average cost per visitor of US$6,858.[38] It also showed that between the fiscal years of 1984 and 1985 (when the ANZUS row erupted) the money allocated to the USIA for such visitors increased by 122 per cent.[39] The USIA officer at the American Embassy in Wellington

36. Quoted in McLaughlin, 'The Campaign to set New Zealand Thinking the USA Way'.
37. Cited in Nicky Hager 'The Role of the USIA and American Embassy in Wellington', unpublished paper, Peace Movement Aotearoa, Wellington, 1987. See also McLaughlin. 'The Campaign to Set New Zealand Thinking the USA Way', p. 5.
38. Cited in Karen Brown, 'On US Embassy's Visitor Programme', *The Evening Post*, 6 December 1986.
39. Ibid.

described the type of people invited to take part in these IV Programs (IVP) as those who 'now, or in the foreseeable future are very likely to be making a substantial contribution to the society and culture of their country'.[40] To this end, by far the majority of New Zealand recipients of USIA grants fell into the category of media journalists and presenters, academics, politicians, trade unionists and political researchers. When the list of recipients of such grants was published, it generated some public debate in New Zealand concerning the ethics of journalists accepting free trips sponsored by a government agency. Indeed, just as the head of current affairs at TVNZ, John Scully, had refused to allow further Worldnet satellite broadcasts, he also clamped down on study visits by his staff paid for by the USIA: 'In general I say no to freebies at a government's expense. If it's under the aegis of a particular government, I suspect that that government may try indirectly to influence opinion by a particular type of exposure at the time, or later down the track.'[41]

It is, of course, extremely difficult to determine how much influence the IV Programs have on those who go on them. Without doubt, many of those New Zealanders who over the years have taken up the USIA's offer of an all-expenses paid trip to the United States have not on their return espoused particularly pro-American views on foreign policy, but there are also clear examples of those who have.

After a month-long trip to the United States in late 1985 under the IV Program, Christchurch college lecturer Stanley Newman returned to New Zealand and established the pro-ANZUS Plains Club which included among its activities the placing of a 'ready to clip and post' coupon in Christchurch newspapers to be sent as a submission to the Defence Committee of Enquiry.[42] The Plains Club, though low on membership, has never, it seems, been low on funds. During the 1987 general election campaign, for example, the group took out full page advertisements in daily papers urging voters to return New Zealand to the Western alliance by voting for the National Party. Just where this money came from is obviously open to some speculation.

Another IVP recipient was Rick Vallence, the President of the Wairarapa province of the Federated Farmers. On his return to New Zealand he gained considerable publicity for his opinion that the Labour government had made a 'huge mis-calculation' in assessing the effects of the ships-ban

40. Ibid.
41. Quoted in McLaughlin, 'The Campaign to Set New Zealand Thinking the USA Way'.
42. Ibid.

policy.[43] Vallence also established the pro-ANZUS 'Wairarapa' group, later re-named Collective Security Inc.

A full list of the IVP recipients would be largely meaningless except to a New Zealand audience, but perhaps of particular interest to us here is the fact that one of the journalists who accepted an IVP trip in 1985 was Stuart McMillan whom we referred to earlier (see p. 112). In 1987 McMillan had the first book on the ships-ban published and in it he adopts a largely pro-American stance on the dispute.[44]

It is difficult to draw hard and fast conclusions concerning the International Visitor Program of the USIA. To accuse it of being a propaganda front for the United States which serves merely to inculcate American beliefs including those of a foreign policy nature on its recipients, is also to question (however implicitly) the integrity of those who choose to accept an IVP trip. But without doubt, the IVP does have a tangible influence on many of those who go on its programmes; why else would the USIA finance it worldwide? Indeed, the Director of the USIA under the Reagan administration, Charles Wick, admitted as much himself. In a statement accompanying the USIA 1987 budget request, Wick wrote that:

> A Bolivian scholar who had been a leading leftist critic of this country [the USA] returned from her 30 day International Visitor Program to the U.S. to express praise and admiration for Americans and American institutions. . . . Our foreign service officers frequently tell us that dollar-for-dollar this exchange program is one of the most effective at any price in terms of enhancing public diplomacy and erasing cultural misperceptions.[45]

The American Participants (AMPART) Program

The International Visitor Program of the USIA which sends New Zealanders to the United States is complemented by the American Participants (AMPART) Program which pays for American academics, business people, government officials and media people to visit foreign countries, including New Zealand, on speaking tours or 'fact-finding' missions.

43. Ibid. On the Plains Club and ANZUS 'Wairarapa' group see Karen Brown, 'On US Embassy's Visitor Programme', *The Evening Post*, 24 December 1986.
44. McMillan, *Neither Confirm Nor Deny*.
45. Cited in Hager, 'The Role of the USIA'.

According to the USIA's 1986 annual report, 'each USIA post, as part of its Country Plan, requests speakers on various topics that support US objectives in that country'.[46]

Again, due to the Freedom of Information Act, a 'Calendar of Actions Planned' by AMPART visitors to New Zealand in 1986 was released and revealed the extent to which the ships-ban/ANZUS dispute was given priority by the USIA. Of the seven entries listed specifically as AMPART Programs, five were concerned with security/nuclear/Soviet matters in the Pacific.[47] But this is just the tip of the iceberg. Also mentioned, for example, was a planned 'intensified speakers' programme between May and December, the participants of which were not listed,[48] and US Ambassador Paul Cleveland was to embark on a series of speeches on 'bilateral issues'.[49] One planned event which did not take place was another Worldnet satellite programme featuring both Australian and US defence experts, and to be shown in New Zealand 'if appropriate'. It is not difficult to deduce what the message of this programme would have been.

Claims that the AMPART visitor programmes are primarily cultural exchanges in many fields including journalism, the arts, politics, education and so on, would carry more credibility were it not for the fact that in 1986, according to the USIA 'Calendar of Actions Planned', only the sponsored tour of the Ellis Marsalis jazz quartet could truly be construed primarily as a 'cultural' visit.[50]

Courting Journalists: The USIA in Wellington

Another controversial activity undertaken by the United States Embassy in Wellington (with USIA funding) was the attempt to win influence in the New Zealand media by the wining and dining of prominent political journalists and editorial staff. The evidence of such activities has come from a few of the journalists themselves, and for this reason no accredited sources are named. But the information has been disclosed to Wellington peace activist Nicky Hager who has extensively documented the details in an unpublished paper.[51] According to Hager, US Ambassador Paul

46. Quoted in ibid.
47. 'Calendar of Events and Actions Planned' (USIA 1986), cited in ibid.
48. Hager, ibid.
49. Ibid.
50. Ibid.
51. Ibid.

Cleveland and Wellington USIA officer Mike Gould arranged informal 'discussion/background briefings' for journalists at Cleveland's Wellington home. The informal meetings were strictly 'off the record', and typically called when there was a message that the Americans wanted to give about forthcoming or recent events. Of course, the meetings also allowed for personal contacts to be built up, and went a long way to explaining the root of 'unnamed sources in Wellington', or 'well placed sources' which appeared in the New Zealand press when controversy over the ships-ban or any other issue reigned. Less selective dinners and drinks were arranged at the American Embassy, and at restaurant lunches organised by Gould. According to Hager: 'The only comparable activities organised by other embassies in New Zealand are much more open and less selective receptions organised to commemorate special days or meet overseas visitors.'[52]

The seriousness with which the United States viewed New Zealand's nuclear-free policies was highlighted by the revelation that in May 1986 the National Security Council had instructed the USIA to lead a 'government wide public affairs strategy' addressing the nuclear-free legislation which was before the New Zealand Parliament.[53] In a submission to the House of Representatives Appropriations Sub-committee, and reviewing its 1985 and 1986 programmes, the Agency said: 'The questions that are raised in New Zealand are central to our relations with all South Pacific countries. Other nations will find it difficult to resist pressures to emulate the implications of the New Zealand policy.'[54] The controversial Worldnet satellite interactives were also mentioned in the USIA submission as helping to explain US policies, and the opening of a USIA branch post at the Operation Deep Freeze base in Christchurch was described as 'complementing the strategy'.[55]

The news of the USIA campaign to undermine support for the nuclear-free policies in New Zealand met with a barrage of criticism, not least from Deputy Prime Minister Geoffrey Palmer, who said that New Zealanders would not change their views on the anti-nuclear policy 'at the bidding of a foreign power'.[56] However, David Lange was largely silent on the issue – arising as it did at a time when he was attempting to play down the dispute with the United States. For his part, the US State Department

52. Ibid.
53. See, for example, 'US Campaign to Subvert NZ N-Free Policies', *The Press*, 22 May 1986.
54. Cited in McLaughlin, 'The Campaign to Set New Zealand Thinking the US Way'.
55. 'US Campaign to Subvert NZ N-Free Policies', p. 4.
56. Quoted in 'PM Stays Silent on US War of Words', *The Dominion*, 24 May 1986.

spokesperson Bernard Kalb claimed to be 'puzzled' and 'distressed' at the concern in New Zealand that the US was presenting it views to the people via the USIA.[57]

US Action Against a Nuclear-Free Pacific

Aside from the IV and AMPART Programs, the USIA and similar United States government agencies are involved in other attempts to influence opinion and diminish support for a nuclear-free Pacific. This activity, of course, extends far beyond the shores of New Zealand, and is worthy of a much greater examination than that which can be given here. Summarised below, however, are a few of the activities by these US backed and financed organisations which have been established to promote the pro-American line in various forums in the Pacific.

With a grant of US$300,000 from the USIA in 1983, the now defunct Labour Committee for Pacific Affairs was formed. Its declared aim was to sponsor overseas trips for Australian and New Zealand trade unionists. The Australian Council of Trade Unionists (ACTU) and the New Zealand Federation of Labour (NZFOL) both saw the Committee as an attempt to undermine and counter the strongly anti-nuclear Pacific Trade Union Forum.[58]

In 1986, the *Sydney Morning Herald* revealed that the National Endowment for Democracy (NED) – a body set up by the Reagan administration – had been funded to the tune of one million dollars for the years 1984–5.[59] The most significant activity of the NED is to inject funds into projects which aim to bring 'American-style' trade unionism to the South Pacific from its office in Suva, Fiji.

The establishment of this union office, from which another USIA beneficiary, the Asian-America Free Labor Institute (AAFLI), also operates, followed the nuclear ships ban in New Zealand, and the US perception of a Soviet threat in the Pacific.[60]

Internal AAFLI documents obtained under the Freedom of Information Act reveal the strategy which lies behind the organisation. Refer-

57. Cited in McLaughlin, 'The Campaign to Set New Zealand Thinking the US Way'.
58. See, 'The U.S. Information Service: Agency for Subversion', *New Zealand Monthly Review*, September 1986.
59. David McKnight, 'US Targets Our Anti-Nuclear Unions', *The Sydney Morning Herald*, 17 May 1986.
60. Ibid.

ring to a regional trade union conference in March 1985 an AAFLI report says:

> The Australian and New Zealand representative attempted to gain approval for a political resolution endorsing a pacific nuclear freeze [sic] zone, and supporting New Zealand in its dispute with the US. However, only the South Pacific delegate spoke up in favour of this approach and the conference rejected it. *This was in no small measure due to the close collaboration and friendship nurtured between AAFLI and the South Pacific trade union leaders.* (Our emphasis.)[61]

From its inception, the National Endowment for Democracy has been dogged by controversy, and there have been attempts by the US House of Representatives to reduce its budget in the wake of criticism that it has amounted to a slush fund for conservative groups. In June 1986, it was revealed that the NED was also being used to channel money to the Pacific Democratic Union (PDU) – an alliance of right-wing political parties in the Pacific region. The submission requesting money for the PDU proposed that it be given to 'appropriate' political parties in the Pacific as a means of promoting 'democratic' institutions.[62] The National Party in New Zealand is a member of the PDU and there has been speculation that it has received funds particularly during general election campaigns.

Even this cursory look at some of the US sponsored organisations in the Pacific region reveals a complex web of linkages and secrecy. There are frequent claims that the National Endowment for Democracy provides a cover for CIA operations in the Pacific, and just as frequent denials.[63] But what is abundantly clear is that through various channels and with considerable funds the US authorities are determined to stem the anti-nuclear tide not just in New Zealand but throughout the Pacific region.

A New US Ambassador in Wellington

The attempts to discredit and ultimately overturn the nuclear ships ban in New Zealand in 1986 were not confined to the overt activities of the USIA but included the appointment of a new American ambassador to the

61. Ibid.
62. Hager, 'The Role of the USIA'.
63. See 'The U.S. Information Service: Agency for Subversion'.

country, more high-level military reprisals, and two possible covert attempts to undermine the ships-ban. It is to these efforts that we now turn.

The year had got off to an interesting start when Paul Cleveland was appointed as the new US Ambassador to New Zealand, taking over from H. Monroe Browne. Cleveland was only the third career diplomat (as opposed to political appointee) ever to be assigned to New Zealand, and was transferred from Seoul, where he was Deputy Chief of Mission.

The traditional appointment of American ambassadors to New Zealand as a 'reward' for their service, and as somewhere to while away their twilight years, was clearly not applicable in the case of Paul Cleveland. His appointment led to speculation that he would be at the forefront of a renewed effort to overturn the nuclear ships ban, and he admitted as much in his first press conference when he spoke of the 'essentiality' of restoring port access for American warships.[64] For several months Cleveland kept a low profile on the ANZUS/ships-ban dispute, preferring to 'look and listen and find out how things are here and how people feel about the issue'.[65] His quiet diplomacy was not to last, however, and, as we shall see later, his contributions to the ANZUS debate were sometimes a little less than subtle.

At the same time as Cleveland arrived in Wellington, a new US ambassador was also appointed to the post at Canberra. Just five weeks after taking up the position, William Lane shocked Australian journalists at his first press conference when he said that New Zealand was being 'punished for being a bad boy' by the United States.[66] The United States, he said, planned 'to do many things' to persuade New Zealand to reverse the nuclear ships ban.[67] Within a day, the State Department refuted the claims made by Lane, and said that the US had 'readjusted' its defence and security ties with New Zealand, but was not punishing the country.[68] The State Department also denied claims that there was a deliberate linkage in the timing of Lane's comments and those of US Navy Secretary John Lehman who called the ships-ban 'outrageous' and the 'height of irresponsibility'.[69]

---

64. Jane Clifton, 'Port Access Priority for New Ambassador', *The Dominion*, 9 January 1986.
65. Ibid.
66. Peter Costigan, 'NZ Punished, Says US Diplomat', *The Dominion*, 8 February 1986.
67. Quoted in Denis Grant, 'Break in Crony Inheritance', *New Zealand Sunday Times*, 5 January 1986.
68. Tom Bridgman, 'US Envoy Lane Erred With Bad Boy NZ Talk', *The Evening Post*, 11 February 1986.
69. Quoted in ibid.

In the early months of 1986 it appeared that New Zealand was becoming a southern summer retreat for members of the US Congress and Senate. In January Stephen Solarz (the Head of the House of Representatives Foreign Affairs Sub-committee on Asia and the Pacific) visited Wellington for talks with David Lange, and he was quickly followed by a twelve-person delegation from the Armed Services Committee of Congress. One of the delegation, Republican Herbert Bateman, was given space in the Christchurch *Press* newspaper to vent his distate at the ships-ban and the Labour government: 'The people of New Zealand deserve and need to know that it is unrealistic, impractical and erroneous for your Government to tell you that can keep your present policies and keep and maintain your ANZUS Pact partnership.'[70]

No less critical was the US Secretary of Defense, Caspar Weinberger, who announced that New Zealand would not be on his itinerary during a Pacific and Asia tour in March.[71] And it was reported from Washington that James Kelly, the Deputy Assistant Secretary of Defense for East Asia and Pacific Affairs and a hardline critic of New Zealand, had been chosen to succeed Dr Gaston Sigur as advisor to President Reagan on Asia and the Pacific in the National Security Council.[72] In turn, Gaston Sigur (no dove himself) was appointed as the Assistant Secretary of State for East Asian and Pacific Affairs, taking over from Paul Wolfowitz who was appointed as Ambassador to Indonesia.[73]

In March, the US Arms Control and Disarmament Agency deputy head, David Emery, payed his third visit to New Zealand in two years, and predicted that the US and Soviet Union could achieve cuts of 50 per cent in their nuclear arsenals during negotiations at Geneva. Although he did not specifically criticise New Zealand's nuclear-free policies, it did not take too much of an imagination to realise that his underlying theme was that the 'West' must stay united in its dealings with the Soviets. Any perceived fragmentation of alliances would put in jeopardy possible arms control agreements by removing the Soviet incentive to negotiate.[74]

Further visitors from United States officialdom to New Zealand included a former Republican senator, Charles Percy. He was particularly concerned with the nuclear-free legislation before Parliament and, whether by accident or design, his declaration after reading the legislation

70. Herbert H. Bateman, 'American View of Treaty's Future', *The Press*, 17 February 1986.
71. 'Weinberger Stays Away', *The Dominion*, 26 February 1986.
72. Ibid.
73. Richard Long, 'Hardliner Tipped as NZ Watchdog', *The Dominion*, 7 March 1986.
74. See Roger Mackay, 'Arms Cuts . . .', *The Evening Post*, 6 March 1986.

that 'a lot of it can stay intact', must have raised a good many eyebrows, if not hackles in New Zealand.[75]

It was in 1986 that the first of two possible examples of CIA-backed covert attempts to undermine the ships-ban came to light. The first, in February, was associated with the sighting of a submarine in the territorial waters of the Cook Islands – for which New Zealand assumes certain defence responsibilities under a compact of free association. The second, in December, concerned a massive loans scam which was in many ways similar to the loans scandal which led to the downfall in 1975 of the Whitlam government in Australia. The loans scam will be discussed later in this chapter, but here it is worthwhile outlining the story of what proved to be a tantalisingly elusive submarine, because it came to light at a time of much activity on the part of the USA to discredit the Labour government and overturn the ships-ban.

When peace movement activists suggested that the CIA might attempt to destabilise the government in New Zealand their claim was viewed by many people as a somewhat bizarre form of paranoia, so at this juncture it is worthwhile pointing out that there is already incontrovertible evidence that the CIA had been active in New Zealand even before the nuclear ships ban. In 1978 the CIA established a business front company for deep-cover operations in New Zealand. This fact was revealed by the New Zealand *National Business Review* in March 1985.[76] The company, named Bishop, Baldwin, Rewald, Dillingham and Wong Ltd (BBRDW), was established as a 'cover' for 'CIA agents posing as businessmʾn while gathering political and economic intelligence'.[77] This cover was only 'blown' after the collapse of BBRDW's parent company in Honolulu, and a $34m fraud case ensued. There is not room here to detail the exposé of BBRDW in New Zealand, but it is important to acknowledge the very real possibility of covert attempts to undermine the nuclear ships ban.

Elusive Submarines . . .

On 17 February, two Cook islanders spotted the periscope and bow wave of a submarine from an aircraft in which they were flying. Three days later

---

75. Quoted in 'US Visitor Calls for Bill Changes', *The Dominion*, 7 March 1986.
76. Warren Berryman, 'CIA Company for "Cover" Here', *National Business Review*, vol. 16, no. 8 (Issue 614), 11 March 1985, p. 1–2.
77. Ibid.

two people fishing off the Cooks witnessed a conning-tower surface only about 100 metres from their boat. After telling the police, a search by two New Zealand Royal Air Force *Orions* was begun using sonobouys to detect and monitor any submarine noises. From the government of the Cooks, but more so from the government in New Zealand, there followed a series of statements and reports which lent confusion and contradiction to the whole incident.

In a painstakingly researched paper, New Zealand peace researcher Owen Wilkes has detailed the sequence of events as they occurred.[78] He postulates the theory that the submarine was most likely a US Navy boat masquerading as a Soviet one in order to fuel the fear of a 'Soviet threat' in the Pacific, and thus undermine the nuclear-free policy of New Zealand.

The evidence cited by Wilkes is convincing. A series of 'leaks', retracted statements, and obvious discomfort on the part of the New Zealand government, the Chief of Defence Staff, and the US Embassy in Wellington strongly suggested that the submarine had been not only detected by the New Zealand *Orions*, but also identified. Had, for example, Lange declared that the submarine could not be identified per se, the matter might have rested, but he released information that the submarine had been detected but was not being tracked by the *Orions*. As Wilkes suggests, given the past history of Soviet ships being tracked by New Zealand aircraft for anything up to two weeks, it was something of a surprise that the submarine should not have been followed.

By not tracking the submarine, Lange was inadvertently declaring that the submarine was not seen as a threat.[79] Later, Lange claimed that the submarine could not be positively identified – which begged the question of why it was *not* followed until such time as it could be. As Wilkes so aptly states:

> the behaviour of the submarine – travelling on the surface in broad daylight at speeds fast enough to create a bow wave, in the vicinity of an aircraft and fishermen, on two occasions 3 days apart, within territorial waters, and loitering a further few hours until detected by an Orion – was the behaviour of a submarine that was intended to be detected. . . . There was no conceivable reason why the Soviet Union would want one of its submarines discovered in the Cook Islands territorial waters.

78. Owen Wilkes, 'Stooging Around the Cook Islands – The Mysterious Case of the Disappearing Submarine', *New Zealand Monthly Review*, vol. XXVII, no. 292, October 1986, pp. 3–13.
79. See ibid., p. 5

Numerous US objectives would however be served if it were *believed* that a Soviet submarine had been lurking around the Cooks. . . .[80]

This point was re-iterated by a former CIA agent, Ralph McGehee, during a lecture tour of New Zealand in August 1986. He argued that the country had become a prime target for CIA operations, and said: 'One of the first things is creating a major threat. We find that Russian submarines are coming to the South Pacific. They are seen near the Cook Islands. They are the focus of articles in defence magazines. . . . You use people to keep the pot boiling. . . .'[81]

It is also worth recalling that in their 1984 report for the right-wing and influential Pacific Forum (cited earlier in Chapter 5), Lloyd Vasey and Henry Albinski drew up a list of suggested American responses to the (as then) untested nuclear-free policies of the new Labour government. In the concluding section of their report, headed 'Recommended United States Policies', the authors wrote: 'In broad terms, the United States should review and as feasible improve upon its information and persuasion effort in Australia and New Zealand. . . . It for example might be useful, consistent with security considerations to bring to Australian and New Zealand public attention such facts as Soviet submarine deployments in their neighbourhoods.'[82]

If the submarine spotted off the Cooks was an example of a US covert operation to undermine the nuclear-free policies, it failed only by chance. Wilkes suggests that because the media and political response to the first sighting was not emphatic, the submarine surfaced again three days later. It was sheer coincidence that a Royal New Zealand Air Force *Orion* was at Rarotonga airport (in the Cook Islands) at this time, and thus able to start searching for the submarine quicker than expected. According to Wilkes: 'The Orion not only detected the submarine, which would have been fine from the US viewpoint, and may have even been in the script, but also identified it correctly, which very definitely was not in the script.'[83]

One of the questions which remains is the refusal of Lange to 'come clean' and make public what he knew of the incident. There would, for example, have been tremendous political capital to be gained in disclosing that it was an American submarine posing as a Soviet one. A number of

80. Ibid.
81. Quoted in 'CIA Feared at Work Here', *Nelson Evening Mail*, 16 August 1986.
82. Lloyd R. Vasey and Henry S. Albinski, *Pacific Forum: Australia – New Zealand Trip Report*, published by the *Pacific Forum*, January 1985, p. 17.
83. Wilkes, 'Stooging Around the Cook Islands', p. 13.

possibilities explain why he did not do so. It is possible that Lange was determined to avoid more US antagonism towards his government, there may be secret agreements forbidding New Zealand from disclosing US submarine movements, or it could be that he used the incident as a 'bargaining chip' with the Americans in future talks over ANZUS.[84]

Whatever the truth may be, many questions remain unanswered to this day. Although one should be wary of immediately alleging the hand of the CIA at work, given the evidence (and the apparent reluctance to contradict it), such a conclusion is difficult to avoid.

The ANZUS/ships-ban dispute was to reach a watershed in June 1986 when George Shultz and David Lange met for talks during an Association of South-East Asian Nations (ASEAN) meeting in Manila. That meeting, and its consequences, will be discussed shortly, but before doing so it will be valuable to look at some of the events preceding it, and in particular the efforts of Britain to persuade Lange to compromise on the nuclear-free policies.

Tugging Colonial Heartstrings: The Royal Navy and Britain

In December 1985, the *Observer* newspaper in London had disclosed that the Royal Navy would be taking the place of New Zealand in the US *Rimpac* naval exercises in the Pacific from mid-May to the end of June.[85] By early 1986 it became clear that the British fleet (operating under the codename *Global 86*) would consist of seven vessels – six of which would undoubtedly be 'nuclear-capable', and would be in the Pacific Ocean for approximately eight months. Speculation that Britain would test the nuclear-free policy of New Zealand by requesting port facilities was fuelled by the announcement that British Admiral of the Fleet and Chief of Defence Staff, Sir John Fieldhouse, would visit the country in February to discuss 'subjects of mutual concern, and to demonstrate Britain's continuing interest in the [Pacific] area'.[86] It transpired that no request for port facilities was forthcoming, but Fieldhouse used his visit to test the political water on the matter. He also wasted little time in criticising the nuclear-free legislation, and warned that its enactment could result in

84. These conclusions were among those drawn by Wilkes, ibid., p. 13.
85. Cited in 'Britain to "Join" Rimpac Exercise', *The Evening Post*, 16 December 1985.
86. Quoted in Murray McLaughlin, 'Britain's Top Admiral to Visit NZ', *The Dominion*, 31 January 1986.

British defence co-operation, training and intelligence information with New Zealand being restricted.[87] The media reported that this was the first time that Britain had been so forthright in opposing the nuclear-free policies and legislation.[88]

Specifically on the nuclear ships ban, Admiral Fieldhouse attempted to pull at a few colonial heartstrings when he brooded that: 'We won't attempt to go where we are not welcome.'[89] So it was hardly a surprise when in March 1986 the British High Commissioner in Wellington, Terrence O'Leary, announced that the Royal Navy would not be visiting New Zealand during the *Rimpac* exercises and *Global 86* deployment.[90]

However, the British did not let the matter rest there, and in April the Minister of State, Foreign and Commonwealth Office, Baroness Young, arrived in New Zealand for talks with officials and to warn of 'adverse consequences' if the anti-nuclear legislation was passed:[91]

> If legislation were passed here which we judged to be in conflict with our "neither confirm nor deny" policy, it would be bound to have adverse consequences . . . it would not be possible for ships of the Royal Navy to visit New Zealand. . . . The cessation of naval visits would in turn inevitably lead to some loosening of the close and special ties between the United Kingdom and New Zealand. . . . We would deeply deplore this change.[92]

By her own admission, Baroness Young said that British discussions with the New Zealand government were designed to make New Zealand's legislation compatible with the British neither-confirm-nor-deny policy.[93] There was, it seems, no question of making the British policy compatible with the nuclear-free legislation.

When Baroness Young returned to Britain empty-handed, the implicit threats to New Zealand's export trade with Britain and the EEC were

87. Richard Long, 'British Aid "Endangered" by Nuke Law', *The Dominion*, 20 February 1986.
88. See, for example Richard Long, 'British Nuke Ban Position Spelt Out', *The Dominion*, 19 February 1986.
89. Quoted in ibid.
90. 'Royal Navy Snubbing No-Nuke NZ', *The Dominion* 29 March 1986.
91. See Karen Brown, 'Nuke-Ships Ban Will Loosen UK–NZ Links: Lady Young', *The Evening Post*, 9 April 1986.
92. Quoted in Baroness Lady Young, 'Old Friends on Different Paths: The British Viewpoint' (taken from an address to the Wellington branch of the New Zealand Institute of International Affairs, 8 April 1986), *New Zealand International Review*, vol. XI, no. 4, July/August 1986, pp. 20–2.
93. See Brown, 'Nuke-Ships Ban Will Loosen UK–NZ Links'.

given a higher profile. Until now, Britain had remained largely silent on the matter of trade reprisals, but in late April British High Commissioner Terence O'Leary was again given the task of conveying the message from London: 'Sometimes your spokesmen seem to forget that your largest trading market is still Western Europe, not North America, not Japan, and not Australia.'[94]

It is true that only two months later British Deputy Trade Minister Alan Clark gave assurances that Britain would continue to support New Zealand's case in Europe in spite of the differences between the two countries on the nuclear issue.[95] But the purpose of such seemingly conflicting statements was to create uncertainty in the minds of New Zealand business people and government officials, as well as appealing to the pro-British sentiment still found in many New Zealanders.

Lange Lambasts the Americans and British

We saw in the previous chapter how David Lange became more forthright in his criticism of the American response to the ships-ban. In May 1986 his growing anger at the Reagan administration was vented in a speech he delivered to the Auckland regional conference of the New Zealand Labour Party. Any doubts regarding his commitment to the nuclear-free policies were wholly dismissed by the content of his speech, which was a passionate defence of New Zealand's nuclear-free stance, and a damning indictment of the responses of the Americans and British. The following passages taken from the speech amply illustrate the point:

> We believe that the fate of the world should not be the exclusive property of the nuclear powers. It is ... outrageous to us that the defence of Western Europe is based on NATO's promise to blow up the world. . . . They have no right to decide the fate of all the rest of us.[96]

> Some of the jeremiahs of the right were saying last year that if the government maintained its independent course New Zealand would be reduced to a client state. That is ironic. That is exactly what we were before. We are not now and will not be again. . . .[97]

94. Quoted in 'British Warning on Link', *The Dominion*, 3 April 1986.
95. Cited in 'Nuke Policy No Problem', *The Evening Post*, 7 June 1986.
96. David Lange (speech notes), New Zealand Labour Party Auckland Regional Conference, 9 May 1986.
97. Ibid.

The British sent an admiral out to lecture us this year. Some of the press here seemed to think that they had a right to do that and that we should take him seriously. We are not a colony.[98]

We have explained that New Zealand does not want to be defended by nuclear weapons . . . that we accept responsibility for our defence . . . that we would like some reciprocal assistance in regional security. . . . All of that has come unstuck on the fact the US sees the ANZUS alliance in terms of the global projections of its nuclear power. . . . If that is all there is to ANZUS there is no point in New Zealand being in it.[99]

I think it would be a remarkable step forward in the cause of disarmament if the United States agreed to remove its nuclear presence from the South Pacific. If we are serious about rolling back the tide of nuclear escalation this is surely the place to start. We have started in New Zealand and we shall not give up.[100]

Lange's speech came on the eve of his departure for a tour of Europe, which included a keynote address to the world congress in Cologne of the International Physicians for the Prevention of Nuclear War. However, after his Auckland speech, diplomatic representatives of the United States and West Germany informed the New Zealand Ministry of Foreign Affairs that if Lange delivered a similar speech to the physicians' congress, they would consider withdrawing their ambassadors from Wellington.[101] The heavy-handed pressure worked, and Lange's address to the conference was a major disappointment to many onlookers. New Zealand, he said, was not knocking over nuclear dominos, was in a unique position to take the action it had, and understood the 'brave and weighty' reasons why other countries in Europe had 'gone down the nuclear path'.[102]

The New Zealand Prime Minister's trip to Europe was dubbed a fortnight of 'concentrated diplomacy' by one newspaper reporter.[103] In meetings with Margaret Thatcher and Geoffrey Howe in London, the nuclear-free legislation was top of the agenda, and although no mutually agreeable formula to allow British warship visits to continue was found,

98. Ibid.
99. Ibid.
100. Ibid.
101. See Kevin P. Clements, 'New Zealand Paying for Nuclear Ban', *The Bulletin of the Atomic Scientists*, July/August 1987, p. 42. Also McMillan, *Neither Confirm Nor Deny*, p. 105.
102. Peter O'Hara, 'NZ Not Knocking Over Nuclear Dominos: PM', *The Evening Post*, 4 June 1986.
103. Idem, 'Lange's Key Meeting', *The Dominion*, 9 June 1986.

the atmosphere was generally cordial. One problem occurred, however, when the then British Junior Agriculture Minister John Selwyn Gummer criticised the nuclear ships ban but 'divorced' the present government's actions from the nature of Britain's obligations to the people of New Zealand'.[104] A swift rebuke from Lange accused Gummer of patronising the New Zealand government.[105]

Within a month of returning to New Zealand, Lange was travelling again, this time to the Philippines for a meeting of the ASEAN contries. It was here that he was to meet the US Secretary of State George Shultz to discuss the ANZUS/ships-ban impasse.

Lange and Shultz in Manila

The talks between Lange and Shultz in Manila were something of a watershed in the dispute, although their outcome was a surprise to many observers. It was not widely predicted that Shultz would use the meeting to announce that the United States no longer felt 'obliged' to extend its security guarantee to New Zealand.[106] It had been expected that any such announcement would have been made at the forthcoming meeting of the ANZUS council in San Francisco in August. That Shultz chose Manila rather than San Francisco was almost certainly because he wanted to send a clear message to the Aquino government of the Philippines who had expressed some opposition to the continuing US military presence in the country.

An offer by Lange at Manila to keep secret any refusal of any further proposed US warship visits to New Zealand was turned down by Shultz who said that the Americans would be unable to keep such an agreement secret because, in his words, the US system 'leaked like a sieve'.[107] So it was that on 28 June Shultz declared: 'we part company as friends, but we part company'.[108] The response from Lange was not exactly complimentary, and once again he berated the American refusal to negotiate: 'They have almost heroically refused to engage in negotiation or consultation. . . . At each turn of the tide we have been met by statements of

104. 'Tory Minister Assails Nuke Ban', *The Dominion*, 30 June 1986.
105. Ibid.
106. 'US Rejects NZ Ship Ban Secrecy Offer', *The Dominion*, 30 June 1986.
107. David Porter, 'PM Accuses Shultz Over Anzus Impasse', *The Evening Post*, 30 June 1986.
108. Quoted in James Dallmeyer, 'Speed of US Decision Surprised', *The Evening Post*, 30 June 1986.

133

rejection.'[109]

This angry reaction by Lange was met with a remarkable and unprecedented outburst from the American Embassy in Wellington. A three page 'question and answer' press release was issued in which Lange was accused of 'incorrect' statements, and New Zealand of having a 'nuclear phobia'.[110] Coming from a diplomatic post in a foreign country, the press release trod a very fine line between a legitimate representation of US interests and an illegitimate interference in New Zealand's domestic politics.

Two months after the meeting in Manila, a 'truncated' ANZUS Council meeting was held in San Francisco. Lange predicted that the meeting would 'inevitably' provide a forum for the United States to reiterate the withdrawal of its security guarantee, and a joint communique issued by the US and Australia on 12 August confirmed this. The United States, it said, had 'suspended its security obligations to New Zealand under the ANZUS Treaty, pending adequate corrective measures . . . access for allied ships and aircraft is essential to the effectiveness of the ANZUS alliance. . . . New Zealand's current policies detract from individual and collective capacity to resist armed attack.'[111]

The announcement raised questions about further reprisals designed to induce the 'corrective measures' desired by the United States and Australia. For example, it was not clear if the Americans would continue to supply New Zealand with military equipment at' favourable' prices. But at least one possibility was temporarily laid to rest. The United States 'Operation Deep Freeze' air-base (which is officially only a support facility, and stopping-off point for US military and scientific personnel and equipment travelling to Antarctica) would remain in Christchurch. The nuclear-free legislation provided for a blanket clearance of US C–141 *Starlifter* aircraft using the base; a fact that was to cause controversy during 1987.

In the wake of the San Francisco meeting, the report of the Defence Committee of Enquiry was made public. It had been a quite remarkable example of public consultation on foreign and defence policy, but the conclusions which it drew were often the subject of intense criticism and dispute. In particular, the apparent preference of a majority of New

109. Quoted in 'US Rejects NZ Ship Ban Secrecy Offer'.
110. 'ANZUS – Shultz – Lange Meeting', press release issued by the United States Information Service, Embassy of the United States, Wellington, 2 July 1986.
111. 'Communique From the 35th ANZUS Meeting, San Francisco, 12th August 1986', issued as a press release from the United States Information Service, Embassy of the United States, Wellington, 12 August 1986, paragraph 5.

Zealanders to allow nuclear ship visits to continue if that was the price to pay for remaining in ANZUS was hardly music to the ears of the government.[112] The report was also critical of the government's handling of the dispute with the United States, but by promising that the findings of the Committee would be taken into account in the preparation of a major defence review in 1987, the government went some way to diffusing the situation.

The Voice of the Pro-Nuclear Lobby

If the months after March in 1985 represented something of a consolidation of the nuclear-free policies on the government side, they also represented a period where the pro-nuclear lobby in New Zealand began to find its own voice, even if the words it spoke were largely reiterations of those emanating from Washington.

On 9 October 1985, seventeen former senior military officers in New Zealand issued a joint statement in which they urged the government to reconsider the nuclear ships ban because of the effect the policy was having on the ANZUS alliance. Their statement was widely reported, and apparently followed six months of behind-the-scenes letter writing to · David Lange.[113] Hence their viewpoints were not unknown to Lange, who predicted that the joint statement would do little to enhance their case. Lange is recognised by friend and foe alike as something of a master of the 'one-liner' or 'rejoinder', but he was to suffer from an off-the-cuff description of the former defence chiefs as 'geriatric generals'.[114] Not only was the remark considered insulting, but also – given the fact that his own Minister of Defence was the wrong side of seventy – not entirely appropriate to the occasion either.

The former defence chiefs issued a lengthy statement condemning the nuclear-free policies, and the following quote from it is indicative of their message for Lange's government: 'In the present situation the enactment of the proposed ship-ban legislation . . . would certainly prejudice any possibility of restoring the ANZUS relationship in full. . . . Since no

---

112. See 'Defence and Security: What New Zealanders Want', report of the Defence Committee of Enquiry, July 1986. Government Printer, Wellington, 1986, esp. pp. 42–4.
113. 'N-Free Policy Condemned by Former Forces Chiefs', *New Zealand Herald* (Auckland), 9 October 1985.
114. Ibid.

acceptable compromise seems possible, the current policy should be abandoned.'[115] If nothing else, the severe criticism of the government by the retired servicemen helped to fuel a pro-nuclear campaign by the Returned Service Association and the Army Association in New Zealand.[116]

Also in 1985 Dr Ray Cline, the head of an ANZUS think-tank which was discussed in Chapter 5 (pp. 68–9), visited New Zealand again, giving rise to speculation that he was involved in activating the pro-nuclear domestic opposition to the Labour government.[117] A retired Professor of Political Science in New Zealand, Walter Murphy, set up a local branch of the Professors' World Peace Academy in December. The academy is known to be backed by the Unification Church ('Moonies') worldwide, and through this network is linked with the World Anti-Communist League (WACL) which in turn is known to have links with Cline's ANZUS think-tank.[118] Leading members of the New Zealand National Party, including two MPs, attended a WACL conference in Tonga during September 1985, which promoted the 'communist threat' in the Pacific and paid particular attention to New Zealand and the ANZUS row.[119]

Despite the multi-faceted attacks on the nuclear ships ban from both home and abroad, the policy remained popular in the eyes of a majority of New Zealanders. A public opinion poll taken in September, for example, showed 59 per cent support for the ships-ban, but also a greater percentage (71 per cent) in favour of remaining in ANZUS.[120] Clearly, the 'ANZUS is destroyed' card was the one that opponents of the policies saw as the most likely to swing opinion their way. This fact was not lost on the Reagan administration and the USIA who, as we have already seen, stepped up their efforts to undermine support in New Zealand for the Lange government in 1986.

In addition to those already described in this chapter, other visitors to New Zealand in 1986 who criticised the ships-ban included the UK's top military advisor to NATO, Air Chief Marshal Sir Michael Knight,[121] US Senator Richard Lugar–who claimed that Russian nuclear weapons were

---

115. Quoted in 'Peace and Security Through Strong Collective Defence Arrangements' (text of the joint paper on the ANZUS issue by former defence chiefs), *New Zealand Herald*, 9 October 1985.
116. See Dennis Small, 'The Rise of the Pro-Nuclear Right', *New Zealand Monthly Review*, vol. XXVII, no. 293–4, November/December 1986, pp. 5–8.
117. Ibid.
118. Ibid.
119. Ibid.
120. Peter Freedman, 'Lange on Nuclear Tightrope', *The Dominion*, 27 December 1985.
121. 'UK Nato Chief Arrives', *The Evening Post*, 24 May 1986.

trained on New Zealand, [122] and a delegation of British MPs.[123] Two US academics also poured scorn on the nuclear-free policies. Professor Lucian Pye, during a visit to New Zealand, suggested that a reinvigorated American patriotism would not work in New Zealand's favour,[124] and Richard Fisher, a researcher with the Heritage Foundation, published a report in which he claimed that the hand of Moscow could be seen at work in the New Zealand peace movement.[125]

The domestic pro-nuclear/ANZUS lobby had become more vocal and organised by 1986. In March, a new right-of-centre policy institute was established in New Zealand. Called the New Zealand Centre for Independent Studies, much of its work was to be on economic issues, but according to its founder Max Bradford, defence was a topic that had been 'driven by the left' and needed alternative ideas.[126] At least five new pro-nuclear groups were also established in 1986. These were The Senate, Supporters for ANZUS, The Campaign for a Soviet Free New Zealand, and the previously mentioned Plains Club and ANZUS 'Wairarapa' group (Collective Security Inc.).

In various ways these groups attempted to undermine the nuclear-free policies. Overall, however, the impact of the pro-nuclear groups in New Zealand was minimal. Their membership was small (albeit wealthy) and their influence reflected this. This is not to imply that they could be ignored, or had no influence at all, but simply to suggest that their mass appeal was limited.

Other significant events of 1986 included the ratification of the South Pacific Nuclear Free Zone Treaty in December, when Australia became the eighth country to sign the protocols (only the Soviet Union of the nuclear powers had signed the protocols – the others were still deliberating on the matter). Also in December it was announced that New Zealand would begin withdrawing its 740-strong battalion from Singapore. In the words of David Lange: 'New Zealand now wanted to concentrate its defence effort on New Zealand and the South Pacific.'[128]

---

122. Bernard Lagan, 'NZ Nuke Target, Claims Senator', *The Dominion*, 29 August 1986.
123. 'Lange and UK Reps Discuss Nuke Issue', *The Evening Post*, 9 December 1986.
124. Bernard Lagan, 'Ship Ban Support Slipping, Says Visitor', *The Dominion*, 6 September 1986.
125. Richard Long, 'Antinuclear Push Picked to Rebound', *The Dominion*, 29 July 1986.
126. Fran O'Sullivan, 'Right-Wingers Set up Policy Research Centre', *New Zealand Sunday Times*, 23 March 1986.
127. See Small, 'The Rise of the Pro-Nuclear Right', pp. 5–8.
128. 'NZ Withdraws Military Force From Singapore', *The Evening Post*, 24 December 1986.

The nuclear-free legislation came back to Parliament with no watering down of its ship-ban provisions and passed its reading on a comfortable 44–26 vote.[129]

As 1986 drew to a close, another scandal emerged which, like the elusive submarine off the Cook Islands described earlier, bore many of the hallmarks of a covert attempt to discredit, undermine and perhaps ultimately overturn the Labour government.

On 16 December, National Party MP Winston Peters revealed to Parliament that secret and unauthorised negotiations had been taking place between the Department of Maori Affairs and a consortium of businessmen in Hawaii to secure a substantial loan for investment in Maori business ventures in New Zealand and overseas.[130] The loan talked of was for NZ$600m repayable over a 25-year term at an incredibly low interest rate of 4 per cent. The finders fee, however, was a massive 6 per cent of the total sum (NZ$36m) simply to arrange the loan. An agreement 'in principle' for the loan had been signed in mid-September.

Again, much of the investigative research into the origin of the proposed loan, and the dubious background of its propagators, was carried out by Owen Wilkes.[131] The mainstream media was more concerned with the ramifications of a permanent head of the Department of Maori Affairs undertaking negotiations for what later transpired as a non-existent loan, without the apparent knowledge of his Minister. With a few exceptions, the media were not particularly concerned with the background and motives of those who were behind the loan scam.

As the details of the loan unfolded, it became clear that those behind it were hardly 'respectable' business people in any sense of the word. Indeed, it was disclosed that the so-called source of the loan – an Achmed Omar of Kuwait – did not even exist.[132] Within three days of the disclosure of the loan negotiations, the *Evening Post* in Wellington was calling for a public inquiry into what became dubbed the 'Maori Loans Affair'. 'Too much doubt', an editorial in the paper said, 'is cast on the credibility of Government management.'[133] There were calls for government ministers to resign, and comparisons were made with the 'loans'

129. See Richard Long, 'Anti-nuke Bill Keeps Ship-ban Provision', *The Dominion*, 17 October 1986.
130. Owen Wilkes, 'The CIA and the Honolulu Loan Scam', *New Zealand Monthly Review*, March 1987, pp. 6–7.
131. Ibid.
132. Ibid., p. 6.
133. 'A Case for a Public Enquiry', *The Evening Post*, 19 December 1986.

scandal which ultimately led to the fall in 1975 of the Whitlam government in Australia.[134]

The comparison with Whitlam's downfall was telling. On 24 January 1987, New Zealand Television reporter Bill Ralston suggested that the CIA might have instigated the loans affair in an attempt to destabilise and ultimately topple the Lange government: 'History's shown how the CIA have used money, frauds and political embarrassment to destabilise governments unsympathetic to US policies – Whitlam in Australia, Allende in Chile, the Sandinistas in Nicaragua. . . . The target could now be David Lange and Labour in New Zealand.'[135]

Acting Prime Minister Geoffrey Palmer dismissed such suggestions,[136] but it was later proved that at least two of the people involved who spoke with Maori representatives were proven CIA operatives.[137] Both men (Robert Allen and James Hanna) had been named by American lawyers as being on the payroll of the CIA during the fraud case involving a CIA front company established in Auckland in 1978 and exposed in 1985. Furthermore, there were unconfirmed reports from Honolulu that another of the men involved in the loans scam, Steve Thomas, was the serving professional officer of the CIA in Hawaii.[138]

On 16 February, David Lange acknowledged that some people connected with the Maori loans proposal 'definitely' had CIA connections, but he denied that the organisation itself was involved.[139] For a time the Labour government appeared to lose all credibility, and handled the affair badly. Its saving grace was the fact that Maori Affairs Minister Koro Wetere had stopped the loan deal going ahead. Had he not done so, the chances of the government surviving the affair would have been decidedly slim.

If the loans scam was a CIA covert operation, its intention was clearly to destabilise the government by creating a climate of racial tension surrounding either the denial of funds for Maori business ventures, or (if Wetere had been persuaded to sign for the non-existent loan) by causing a major – and probably terminal – crisis for the government.

The loans affair did indeed bear the hallmarks of just such an operation

---

134. See, for example, Hank Schouten, 'Loan Affair Sank Whitlam', *The Evening Post*, 19 December 1986.
135. 'TV Report Links CIA to Maori Loan Row', *The Evening Post*, 24 January 1987.
136. 'No Evidence of CIA Link', *The Evening Post*, 26 January 1987.
137. 'CIA Destabilising Link Made in Loans Affair', *The Press*, 24 January 1987.
138. Wilkes, 'The CIA and the Honolulu Loan Scam', p. 7.
139. 'CIA Individuals in Loan Row, Says Lange', *The Dominion*, 17 February 1987.

and the fact that conclusive proof does not (as yet) exist, should not detract from the strong circumstantial evidence.

With the nuclear ships ban still in place despite all the attempts to undermine it, and with the popularity of the policy still high with the New Zealand electorate, the Labour government had good reason to feel confident as they entered the 1987 election year. And perhaps the most appropriate, and most revealing words with which to conclude this chapter, were those spoken by US Ambassador Paul Cleveland. In January, it will be recalled, he had promised to look, listen and find out how people thought about the ships-ban and ANZUS dispute in New Zealand. By September he had presumably seen and heard enough to persuade him to reveal his thoughts. 'Sometimes', he said, 'it is more difficult to deal with a messy democracy like New Zealand than with some Asian dictatorships.'[140]

---

140. Quoted in Greg Ansley, 'A restlessness in sleepy hollow', *The Star* (Christchurch), 16 September 1986.

CHAPTER 9

1987: The Election Countdown

When one considers the extensive overt (and quite possibly covert) pressures on New Zealand to revoke the nuclear ships ban, it was a quite remarkable feat of endurance that the policy remained, and that legislation to codify it into law was still before the New Zealand Parliament. The Parliamentary term of a government in New Zealand is only three years, so taking into account the 'snap' election of 1984, the latest that the next general election could be held was September 1987. In fact, it was held on 15 August, and in this chapter we look at some of the events preceding it.

The US authorities continued their criticism of the ships-ban in 1987, with Defense Secretary Caspar Weinberger stating during his budget speech to Congress in January that the ANZUS Treaty now operated in a practical sense only as a bilateral pact between the US and Australia.[1] But the first tangible reprisal by the United States in 1987 was the announcement in early February that a five-yearly 'Memorandum of Understanding on Logistical Support', which had been signed in 1982, would be allowed to lapse when it came up for renewal in June.[2] The agreement had given New Zealand an equal priority to buy American military equipment, and also guaranteed priority of supply to New Zealand in the event of an emergency. The quid pro quo, however, was that New Zealand had

1. Tom Bridgman, 'NZ Wiped says Weinberger', *The Evening Post*, 13 January 1987.
2. Richard Long, 'Reagan Halts NZ Cut-Price Defence', *The Dominion*, 3 February 1987.

to make its logistic resources available to the United States if requested. A statement issued by the US State Department summed up the American mood: 'Changes in the US–NZ defense relationship are indicative of New Zealand's loss of the special relationship it held as a close ally . . . . Consistent with its current defense relationships, New Zealand will be offered only those foreign military sales customer rights normally accorded by the United States to non-allies.'[3]

According to US Defense officials, the non-renewal of the 'Memorandum of Understanding' was the 'biggest nail' in the coffin of New Zealand's ties to ANZUS,[4] and this led to claims that the costs to New Zealand of buying military equipment would rise dramatically.[5] The timing of the announcement was perhaps not entirely coincidental with the imminent publication of the Labour government's much awaited Defence Review.

Also before the Defence Review was published, the Commander-in-Chief of the United States Pacific fleet, Admiral James Lyons, held a press conference in Sydney at which he showed new photographic 'evidence' of a massive Soviet air and naval build up at Cam Ranh Bay.[6] The 'evidence' was not particularly new, nor particularly massive, and astute journalists would have surely questioned why the photographs were released in Sydney rather than the United States. No such questions were asked, but Admiral Lyons achieved impressive column inches in the New Zealand press.

There was also another attempt underway – with President Reagan's backing – to remove New Zealand from military assistance and arms export preferences because of the ANZUS row. Congressman William Broomfield had introduced a Bill to this effect in the House of Representatives in January, and wanted it to be passed 'as an appropriate response' to the pending enactment of the nuclear-free legislation by New Zealand.[7] Considering the fact that since the ANZUS dispute New Zealand had received nothing which might be construed as preferential treatment anyway, and had not requested any United States military assistance, the Bill was largely a symbolic political gesture, but it was another example of the United States sending clear signals to other 'Western' allies who might be tempted to follow the nuclear-free path.

3. Quoted in 'US Decision "Nail in Anzus Coffin"', *The Evening Post*, 3 February 1987.
4. Ibid.
5. 'Arms Cost Rise Tipped', *The Evening Post*, 3 February 1987.
6. See 'Pictures Detail Soviet Buildup', *The Dominion*, 10 February 1987.
7. See 'US Chips Away at NZ's Ally Status', *The Dominion*, 25 February 1987.

There is some justification for saying that subtlety had never been a central feature as far as the United States was concerned in its dealings with New Zealand, but it reached a new 'low' when on the eve of publication of the New Zealand 1987 Defence Review, the US Assistant Secretary of Defense, Richard Armitage, claimed that Moscow was continuing to 'exploit the strong anti-nuclear sentiment . . . in New Zealand'.[8] And he claimed that the island nations of the Pacific viewed with concern the breakdown of ANZUS and recognised that: 'Without the United States as an ally, New Zealand has little military capability to help defend the [Southwest Pacific] region.'[9]

It was well known that the Defence Review would focus on the Pacific-centred defence interests of New Zealand, and that these would be given a higher priority than before. The attempt by Richard Armitage to undermine the review before it was published was perhaps an indication of the American frustration that their efforts to overturn the ships-ban had thus far failed.

The 1987 Defence Review

The publication of the Defence White Paper[10] was the fifth step by the government in promoting debate on defence issues. It followed the earlier publication of a defence discussion paper, the public submissions to the Defence Committee of Enquiry, the public hearings of that enquiry, and the publishing of its final report.

In broad terms, the review emphasised a greater self-reliance and a focus on the South Pacific whilst maintaining a close regional defence co-operation with Australia.

The thirty-eight page review was described as the most fundamental change in defence polices since the Second World War:

> For the first time, we have adopted in formal policy terms the concept that the New Zealand armed forces will have a capability to operate independently, although more probably in concert with Australia, to counter low-level contingencies in our region of direct strategic concern. This represents a major break from the past where the concept of

8. 'USSR Influence Grows in Asia, Pacific, says US', *The Evening Post*, 27 February 1987.
9. 'NZ Incapable of Pacific Defence says Pentagon', *The Dominion*, 27 February 1987.
10. V.R. Ward, 'Defence of New Zealand – Review of Defence Policy 1987', Government Printer, Wellington, 1987.

operations for our armed forces was for each service to be individually a component of a larger allied force operating in a wider sphere.[11]

Reaction to the Defence Review was predictable. The Labour Party and peace movement were largely receptive to it, even though it had discounted the possibility of armed neutrality, and the National Party criticised it on the grounds that it was a 'political document' rather than a defence review.[12] Frank Corner, who chaired the Defence Committee of Enquiry, accused the Review of containing no analysis of the wider strategic setting, of the superpower relationship, or of developments in the Pacific area.[13] And an editorial in *The Dominion* argued that the Review begged 'too many questions', and offered 'too few solutions', thereby effectively leaving New Zealand 'defenceless'.[14]

Just as February 1985 had been a month of intense activity surrounding the refusal to allow the USS *Buchanan* port facilities, so February 1987 was also a month of significant pressures. In addition to the Defence Review, and pressures described above, the month also saw the second reading of the New Zealand Nuclear Free Zone, Disarmament and Arms Control Bill. In a volatile debate, former National Prime Minister Sir Robert Muldoon termed the Bill the 'ANZUS Pact Destruction Bill',[15] and National MP Ruth Richardson claimed that the Bill was a 'pacifist brand of cement that holds this disreputable Government together'.[16] What was lacking on the Opposition benches, however, was anything approaching a coherent explanation of how a National government would keep New Zealand nuclear-free whilst at the same time re-admitting American and British warships to New Zealand ports. Claims by the Opposition that the government was using the nuclear-free Bill to prop up its faltering support had more than a hint of truth in them (it was clear, for example, that the government was holding out until the general election was in sight before passing the legislation), but the National Party assertion that they would keep New Zealand nuclear-free *and* allow warship visits to resume was clearly a case of wishful thinking, or wanton deception.

11. Ibid. Chapter 8, conclusion 8.1, p. 38.
12. Richard Long, 'Defence Questions Remain', *The Dominion*, 27 February 1987.
13. See 'Defence Review Critic Talks of "Tunnel Vision"', *The Evening Post*, 27 February 1987.
14. 'Defending New Zealand', *The Dominion*, 4 March 1987.
15. New Zealand Parliamentary Debates (*Hansard*), Second Session, Forty-First Parliament, 1987, *New Zealand Nuclear Free Zone, Disarmament and Arms Control Bill (2nd Reading)*, p. 6988.
16. Quoted in 'Nats Hammer at Anti-Nuclear Bill', *The Evening Post*, 18 February 1987.

The South Pacific Nuclear Free Zone Treaty had already been ratified, but of the nuclear powers only the Soviet Union had thus far signed the protocols. On 4 February the United States announced that it would not be signing, because it was concerned about the spread of nuclear-free zones and the 'constraining' effect they had on the Western nuclear deterrent.[17] On 10 February China signed the protocols, prompting David Lange to declare that it was a welcome move in 'stark contrast' to the refusal of the United States to sign.[18] Not surprisingly, France refused to sign, and likewise Britain, claiming that the legality and wording of the treaty was open to challenge.[19]

An 'Orchestrated' Attempt to Undermine?

The criticism of the Defence Review continued into early March, and in a quite bizarre post-cabinet press conference, David Lange condemned what he saw as an 'orchestrated' act to undermine it. It was more than sheer coincidence, he said, that the review had been the subject of criticism from four quarters: Opposition leader Jim Bolger (who was in London at the time), Opposition Defence spokesperson Doug Kidd, former Foreign Affairs Secretary Frank Corner, and former Chief of Defence Staff Sir Ewan Jamieson.[20] At the same press conference Lange also strongly criticised the apparent plans of Sir Ewan Jamieson and Frank Corner to speak at a seminar in Washington entitled, 'The Red Orchestra – Instruments of Soviet Policy in the South Pacific', and organised by the conservative Hoover Institute. Lange had a programme for the seminar in which both Sir Ewan and Corner were listed as speakers, but he (or his advisors) had failed to check that they would be attending. It transpired, much to Lange's embarrassment, that both had declined the invitation to speak.

The suggestion by Lange that the seminar formed part of an orchestrated campaign by the United States to present his government's defence stance as somehow being directed from Moscow was probably true, but his unfounded accusations about the attendees were immediately picked up as signs of 'extreme paranoia' by Opposition MPs, and the

17. Tom Bridgman, 'US Outlines its Reasons', *The Evening Post*, 6 February 1987.
18. 'Lange Hails China Over Protocols', *The Dominion*, 12 February 1987.
19. 'UK Confirms Treaty Snub', *New Zealand News UK*, 1 April 1987.
20. Hank Schouten, 'Orchestrated Act to Undermine', *The Evening Post*, 2 March 1987.

organiser of the seminar, a former Australian ambassador to the United States, Owen Harries.[21]

The criticisms of the nuclear-free policies continued unabated, but there were few new reprisals that could be made. Almost everything had been done already. So the criticisms instead made great play of New Zealand's perceived break with the 'Western Alliance'. Once again, Richard Armitage vented his anger at the New Zealand policy, which he declared had 'got to the heart of Western deterrence', and had 'torn the fabric which had held for forty years':[22]

> I think it is not understood by most people in New Zealand the depth of feeling in the United States for New Zealand and the regard held in the Administration and in successive administrations for the views of New Zealand . . . . New Zealand by the virtue of her actions pulled herself out of these discussions and we believe dramatically lessened or weakened the fabric of the alliance. The first Western nation to do so.[23]

It should be noted here that the claims by Armitage were at strict variance with those of the New Zealand government. On many occasions Lange and his ministers had emphasised that New Zealand had not withdrawn from the 'Western' alliance – only from the nuclear alliance. For example, in response to Armitage, the New Zealand Ambassador to Washington, Sir Wallace Rowling, said: 'New Zealand is in fact not only historically part of the Western alliance but remains both philosophically and economically very firmly committed to the Western cause.'[24] There was, however, one other reprisal that the United States could conceivably have taken which would have seriously challenged and undermined the nuclear-free policies.

As was mentioned in the previous chapter, the 'Deep Freeze' American air-base at Harewood (Christchurch) was a stopping-off point for US aircraft and personnel en route to US bases in Antarctica. What was not so widely known was the fact that US aircraft also called there en route to American military bases in Australia. From an economic viewpoint the Harewood base is of some importance – contributing up to NZ$20m per

21. Tom Bridgman, '"Orchestrated Campaign" Denied', *The Evening Post*, 3 March 1987.
22. 'NZ Move "Tore Fabric of Western Alliance"', *Greymouth Evening Star*, 24 March 1987.
23. Quoted in 'NZ Action has "Torn Fabric of West's Defence"', *The Star* (Christchurch), 24 March 1987.
24. Quoted in Tom Bridgman, 'NZ "Anxious" Over Rift With US', *The Star* (Christchurch), 26 March 1987.

annum to the New Zealand economy.[25] So a threat to remove the base is likely to be taken very seriously by any New Zealand government.

Retiring Secretary of the US Navy John Lehman began the rumours when he said that the United States inter-departmental Antarctic Policy Group should be convened to 'look seriously at moving out of Christchurch' in view of the Labour government's nuclear-free legislation.[26] The US Embassy in Wellington denied any intention to move the base, but the rumours paved the way for accusations that the Lange government had two policies: one for naval vessels, the other for aircraft using the Harewood base.

The nuclear-free legislation before Parliament gave a blanket clearance to all American military flights using the Harewood base, prompting Opposition MPs to claim that the government implicitly accepted the US neither-confirm-nor-deny policy – for fear of losing the base.

This was denied by Lange, who said: 'we have one policy which relates to neither ships nor aircraft, but to nuclear weapons'.[27] But the assertion by Lange that the blanket clearance was for aircraft which would only be flying to the Antarctic anyway (and thus not be carrying nuclear weapons) ignored the fact that sometimes as many as half the American aircraft using the base were classed as 'channel flights' – which were not associated with the Antarctic programme at all, but passed through New Zealand from Hawaii to American bases in Australia.[28]

According to the New Zealand Nuclear Free Zone, Disarmament and Arms Control Bill, a New Zealand Prime Minister can only grant approval to the landing in New Zealand of any foreign military aircraft if he/she is satisfied that the aircraft will not be carrying nuclear weapons. As an editorial in *The Evening Post* said: 'American refusal to confirm or deny whether any particular US Navy ship carries nuclear weapons is applied to American aircraft too. So how can the Prime Minister be certain that American aircraft are nuclear-free before he grants them permission to

---

25. Richard Long cites this figure in 'Gov't Accused of Policy Shift', *The Dominion*, 10 April 1987, but although much used, there has never been a detailed breakdown of how the NZ$20m figure was reached. Assuming the figure to be true, it is also unclear how much of this money is of direct benefit to the Christchurch economy. It has been estimated, for example, that up to 75 per cent of this sum is spent on buying fuel from multinational corporations. It is quite possible therefore that perhaps only 10–15 per cent of the NZ$20m finds its way into the Christchurch economy – a sum which would be hardly perceptible were it to be lost due to an American withdrawal from the base.
26. Cited in Chris Moore, 'US Navy Secretary "Sabre Rattling"', *The Press*, 4 April 1987.
27. Quoted in Long, 'Gov't Accused of Policy Shift'.
28. 'PM Called Naive Over Use of Base', *The Evening Post*, 11 April 1987.

land?.'[29] The response from Lange to such questions was not entirely convincing. His main tactic seemed to be to round on the Opposition, accusing them of putting the Harewood base at 'grave risk' by all the publicity over the nuclear/non-nuclear status of the aircraft visiting it.[30]

There are perhaps two conclusions to draw from these arguments. Firstly, on the possibility of the Americans moving the base to Hobart in Tasmania, the geo-strategic circumstances made this *extremely* unlikely. A base as far away from Hawaii as Hobart would cause immense problems for the US in terms of re-fuelling aircraft, and also coping with the sometimes extreme changes of weather which characterise the area. Indeed, in February 1988, the US Ambassador Paul Cleveland again reiterated that there was 'no plan, and I think no danger' that the United States might move the base from New Zealand.[31] Secondly, on the nuclear/non-nuclear status of the aircraft using the base, the facts tend to suggest that there may indeed be a contradiction in the nuclear-free policy. At the very least, one must conclude that the blanket clearance sits rather uncomfortably with the declared nuclear-free policy and legislation.

An Iron Fist in a Velvet Glove?: Geoffrey Howe Pays a Visit

If David Lange's handling of the 'Deep Freeze' controversy was not entirely convincing, the same could not be said of the way he dealt with British Foreign Secretary Sir Geoffrey Howe when he visited New Zealand in late April. For once, the press sided with the New Zealand Prime Minister after Howe had quite blatantly threatened the country with trade reprisals if the nuclear ships ban continued, or the nuclear-free legislation was not amended sufficiently to allow warship visits to continue under the neither-confirm-nor-deny policy.

Earlier British visitors to New Zealand, Admiral John Fieldhouse and Baroness Young, had failed to persuade the Labour government to alter its nuclear-free policy, or amend the legislation, so there was some doubt over the purpose of Sir Geoffrey's visit. It became a lot clearer when he issued a press statement after his arrival in which he described as 'very sad' the decision to enact legislation which would enshrine the nuclear-

---

29. Quoted in 'Harewood Base Tests Policy', *The Evening Post*, 13 April 1987.
30. Richard Long, 'Bolger Puts Base at "Grave Risk"', *The Dominion*, 14 April 1987.
31. Quoted in 'Deep Freeze to Stay in NZ', *New Zealand News UK*, 10 February 1988.

free policies.[32] He continued:

> We [the British] deeply regret the rift in ANZUS not just because it means that old friends have fallen out. We deeply regret your impending non-nuclear legislation, not only because the Royal Navy has had to suspend ship visits. . . . Above all we regret these things because we believe Western security has in the process been diminished. We very much hope it will be possible in the near future to remove this shadow over our relations.[33]

Therein lay the key to his visit. With the New Zealand general election only a matter of months away, Sir Geoffrey clearly intended to use his visit to express the Thatcher government's desire to see the National Party returned to office in New Zealand. To this end he accused the Labour government of taking a 'free lunch' on defence, implying that it wanted the 'benefits' of an alliance without the costs,[34] and said that it would be increasingly difficult for Britain to argue for continued New Zealand access to the European butter market: 'We will do our best, but with your current defence policy, it is a fact of life that your cause is less likely to prevail in a European community, 11 of whose 12 members belong to NATO.'[35]

The diplomatic gloves were off, and Lange responded by unleashing a blistering attack on Howe. The 'free lunch' argument, he said, was 'about three years out of date',[36] and on the problems anticipated with the European community he retorted:

> For anyone to come here and attempt to use the difficulties of the European market as a lever against New Zealand's anti-nuclear policy is to advance an argument which is unsustainable and, more than that, unworthy of the relationships between New Zealand and Europe. It is worse, such is its illogicality that it can only be construed as an attempt to intervene in New Zealand's domestic politics.[37]

Editorials in the New Zealand press backed Lange, and severely criticised Howe. Christchurch paper *The Star*, for example, wrote:

32. Ian Templeton, 'Angry Lange Rounds on Howe', *The Guardian*, 28 April 1987.
33. Ibid.
34. Idem, 'Howe, Lange in Cool Talks', *New Zealand Herald*, 27 April 1987.
35. Tom Scott, 'A Spy and a Fist in a Velvet Glove', *New Zealand News UK*, 13 May 1987.
36. Quoted in Templeton, 'Angry Lange Rounds on Howe'.
37. Idem, 'The Kiss-Off', *New Zealand News UK*, 13 May 1987.

149

If Sir Geoffrey had stayed here longer, or if he had paid greater attention to the development of the New Zealand identity, he would have seen this country is no longer the blindly patriotic little South Seas outpost it once was. There is now an independence and a sense of nationality that make his clumsy attempts at influencing New Zealand's affairs deeply offensive.[38]

The New Zealand *Sunday Star* called Howe's comments 'a blatant threat and deserving of condemnation',[39] and *The Dominion* commented that: '[New Zealanders] proud of their nuclear-free stand . . . will find Sir Geoffrey Howe's barely concealed interference in their election-year politics shocking and distasteful'.[40] As if to rub salt into Geoffrey Howe's wound, Lange also declared that the nuclear-free legislation would be passed in June.

It was clear that a pattern of threats and pressures had emerged at this stage. The military reprisals and threatened trade sanctions had utterly failed to change the Labour government's policies, so arguments pertaining to a New Zealand 'break' with the West were given a higher prominence. There was also an increase in scare stories concerning Soviet ambitions in the Pacific, and in April warnings that Colonel Gadaffi's Libya was seeking a foothold in the region. Indeed, such was the immediacy of the Libyan 'threat' that Sir Geoffrey Howe warned Lange of it on his visit, and then within a fortnight of Howe's departure from the country, Australian Foreign Affairs Minister Bill Hayden made a much publicised 'secret' pre-dawn flight to New Zealand where he warned Lange of Gadaffi's attempt to 'destabilize' the Pacific.[41] Lange downplayed the concern from Canberra, and ruled out breaking diplomatic ties with Tripoli. An editorial in the *Sunday Star* summed up the New Zealand attitude: 'The Australian campaign seems to be motivated by Australia's desire to catch up lost ground as a potential leader in the region and to be seen backing the tough United States anti-Gadaffi line.'[42]

38. 'Howe Wrong' (Editorial), *The Star* (Christchurch). Reprinted in *New Zealand News UK*, 20 May 1987.
39. 'PM Responds' (Editorial), *The Sunday Star*. Reprinted in *New Zealand News UK*, 20 May 1987.
40. Quoted in *The Dominion*, 28 April 1987.
41. 'Alarm Bells Over Libyan Presence', *New Zealand News UK*, 13 May 1987.
42. Quoted in ibid.

A Nuclear-Free Fiji . . . For a Month

There was one event of 1987 beyond New Zealand which cannot be ignored, or its significance over-emphasised. On 12 April, a Labour-led coalition headed by Dr Timoci Bavadra won the Fijian general election, and ended the seventeen-year government of Ratu Sir Kamisese Mara.

One of the priorities of the coalition government was to introduce a ban on nuclear-armed and -powered warships entering Fijian ports. Dr Satendra Nandan, the Coalition's spokesperson on Foreign Affairs, said: 'New Zealand has inspired us over what small nations can do and we want to join it in having a moral voice in the South Pacific.'[43]

For his part, David Lange denied any New Zealand influence in the Fijian policy, but there was widespread speculation that the United States would put pressure on the coalition government to revoke its new ships-ban policy. Editorials in the New Zealand press warned against this, saying that any 'heavy-handed' retaliation by the US would be 'utterly counter-productive'.[44] Barely a month after taking office, the Labour coalition government was ousted in a military coup led by Lieutenant Colonel Rabuka. US involvement in the coup seems likely. Strong circumstantial evidence suggests the presence of five CIA agents in Suva at the time of the coup and, over a longer period of time, the cultivation of Fijian army officers by the US military. Again, there is not room here to detail the evidence, or advance the arguments, but since the coup several articles have been published which document the evidence and allegations.[45]

The coup undoubtedly served the interests of the United States, and although no-one in the US administration would publicly admit as much, an unnamed Pentagon source did reveal to the *Sydney Morning Herald* the feeling of the US military: 'We are kinda delighted. . . . All of a sudden our ships couldn't go to Fiji and now all of a sudden they can. We got a little chuckle about the news. . .'.[46]

Some would argue that what the United States was unable to achieve in New Zealand, it achieved with remarkable speed in Fiji. For this reason if

43. Quoted in David Robie, 'Coalition Promises Fiji Nuke Ban', *The Dominion*, 10 April 1987.
44. 'Fiji: End of an Era' (Editorial), *The Dominion*, 14 April 1987.
45. See, for example, Colin James, 'CIA Plot – Or Not?' (special report written for the New Zealand *Sunday Star*), repr. in *New Zealand News UK*, 5 August 1987, pp. 13–14. Stephanie Mills, 'Fiji Behind the Scenes', *Sanity*, August 1987, pp. 19–20. 'US Involvement in the Fiji Coup D'etat', *Lobster* No. 14, 1987, pp. 30–5. Robert Robertson and Akosita Tamanisau, *Fiji: Shattered Coups*, Pluto Press, Leichhardt, NSW, 1988.
46. Quoted in *The Sydney Morning Herald*, 16 May 1987.

no other, any conclusions that the United States 'failed' in New Zealand to overturn the ships-ban need to be tempered, and seen in the wider context of events elsewhere in the Pacific.

Back in New Zealand, the New Zealand Nuclear Free Zone, Disarmament and Arms Control Bill was passed by Parliament on 4 June with a 39–29 majority, and Lange declared that his government was 'proud that for the first time in 40 years New Zealand has made a fundamental reassessment of what constitutes our security'.[47] Thus, the scene was set for the general election which was called for 15 August. The ban on nuclear ships was once again to be an important (and arguably decisive) feature of the election campaign as Labour sought to be re-elected for a second term of office.

The 1987 General Election

When the election campaign got underway, nuclear issues were not apparently high on the agenda. Rather, the radical free-market economic policies of the Labour government took precedence over most other issues. In its economic policies, the government had turned political allegiances on their head, appealing to the wealthy business community and alienating many of Labour's traditional voters. Indeed, it was the National Party which promised policies of 'putting people first', and defending the interests of working people.[48]

Labour had begun the election campaign with a lead in the opinion polls of anything between 18 and 26 per cent.[49] However, this lead was rapidly whittled away to single figures by the penultimate week of the campaign. It was generally agreed that the nuclear-free policy was the most widely supported of any that the Labour Party had followed, so it should have come as no surprise when at almost the eleventh hour it became the focal-point in the Labour efforts to be re-elected. Lange promised to promote the anti-nuclear message worldwide if re-elected, and expressed the hope that 'others will join us in adopting serious measures of nuclear arms control'.[50]

47. Quoted in 'New Zealand Bans Nuclear Arms', *The Guardian*, 5 June 1987.
48. See David Barber, 'NZ Opposition Makes a Race of it', *The Independent*, 14 August 1987.
49. Cited in David Barber, 'Right Trailing as NZ Election Fight Begins', *The Independent*, 20 July 1987.
50. Quoted in David Barber, 'Lange Promises to Export Anti-Nuclear Campaign', *The Independent*, 7 August 1987.

Inadvertently, the Labour message was helped by three retired New Zealand defence chiefs, who entered the election campaign by urging voters to back any compromise whereby New Zealand would be able to return to ANZUS.[51] Their message took the nuclear ships debate to the centre of the campaign and caused considerable problems for the National Party. For some time, National had been claiming that if elected, they would return New Zealand to ANZUS and remain nuclear-free. Their campaign literature stressed this, as did their newspaper advertisments. What they did not explain, was how they would reconcile being 'nuclear-free' *and* readmitting American and British warships to New Zealand, apart from some rather vague references to a policy which would 'trust' the United States and Britain to respect the nuclear-free policy.

There was no coherent policy on the ANZUS/ships-ban dispute coming from the National Party and instead their leader Jim Bolger attacked Lange personally and claimed that a new Labour government might become non-aligned and open ties with Libya and Cuba.[52] It was debating territory on which Labour arguably felt safest, and they took full advantage with a series of television broadcasts and newspaper advertisments promoting the nuclear-free policies. In a television broadcast that featured atomic test explosions, Lange said that no decision would be watched more closely around the world than how New Zealanders voted on the nuclear issue.[53]

On 15 August, for only the second time in fifty years, the Labour Party won a second successive term in government with a comfortable majority of nineteen seats – three more than at the 1984 election. It was the first time since 1951 that a government in power had improved its majority, despite an average swing against the Labour Party of 2.4 per cent.[54] However, the swing against the government was not even and disguised significant trends. In essence, Labour lost support in its traditional urban working-class electorates whilst at the same time gaining support in the wealthy middle-class electorates that would ordinarily have been considered National Party strongholds. Coupled with this, there was a considerable drop in support for third parties in the election. In 1984 the

51. David Barber, 'NZ Defence Chiefs Enter Election Fray with Anzus Call', *The Independent*, 11 August 1987.
52. '"Geriatric Generals" Fire Shot at Lange, but Miss', *The Guardian*, 11 August 1987.
53. Cited in Richard Long, 'Opposition Strikes Back at Lange on Anti-Nuclear Policy', *The Times*, 15 August 1987.
54. Figures from Jonathan Boston and Keith Jackson, 'The New Zealand General Election of 1987', *Electoral Studies*, vol. 7, no. 1, April 1988, p. 70.

Social Credit Party and the New Zealand Party had picked up 19.8 per cent of the votes between them. In 1987 the New Zealand Party slumped to just 0.3 per cent of the votes (a decrease of 11.9 per cent), whilst the Democrats (formerly Social Credit) fell to 5.7 per cent (a decrease of approximately 2 per cent).[55]

The reasons for the decline in the urban working-class vote for Labour and conversely the significant rise in support for the party in middle-class electorates may be gleaned from the economic policies followed by the Lange government. Since its election in 1984, the government had followed a monetarist economic policy which saw interest rates soar, exchange controls removed, state industries corporatised, government subsidies reduced, the top rates of taxation lowered from 66 to 48 per cent, and the imposition of a goods and sales tax of 10 per cent on almost everything including food, books, newspapers, fuel bills, children's clothes and public transport fares. Collectively known as 'Rogernomics' (after the Finance Minister Roger Douglas), the economic policies alienated even the staunchest Labour supporters. A measure of this disenchantment was illustrated by the disaffiliation of the mineworkers' union from the Labour Party which they had helped to found seventy years previously.

But where Labour had lost its traditional voters, it had also picked up new supporters among the business community who welcomed the removal of price controls and the deregulation of the financial and state sectors. Indeed, the nature of the Labour government's economic policy was such that it could not be 'bettered' by the former bastion of monetarist economics, the National Party. The economic rug had successfully been pulled from beneath the National Party and although the Labour government undoubtedly lost as many votes as it gained because of its economic policies, it could seek some comfort in the fact that most of its absent voters probably abstained rather than voted for the National Party.

The problems that the National Party had in convincing voters that they would be better monetarists than the Labour government had been compounded by the fact that during the past three years the party had experienced two changes of leadership, and had spent almost as much time trying to silence their former Prime Minister Sir Robert Muldoon as they had trying to project the image of a party ready and fit to govern New Zealand. The frequent public pronouncements by Muldoon regarding

55. Ibid., pp. 72–3.

economic policy, which were at a variance with those of his party, served to undermine the leadership of Jim McLay. In early 1986 McLay had been replaced by Jim Bolger in an attempt to project a united party, but Bolger, too, had to suffer the indignity of Sir Robert's continued assertions that an interventionist economic policy should be adopted by the party. By the time of the 1987 election, the National Party were still having difficulties in presenting a united image, and perhaps more importantly distinguishing their economic policies from those of the government. That National leader Jim Bolger chose to launch personal attacks on David Lange rather than on Labour's policies was perhaps indicative of the predicament that the party found itself in. As one commentator has noted: 'National found itself arguing that it was seeking power in order to outdo Labour in implementing National principles which it had itself failed to follow while in power between 1975–84.'[56]

There were, then, a number of factors which enabled the Labour government to be re-elected for a second term in office. Its economic policies won as many new supporters as it lost old ones, and it also benefited from the demise of the Social Credit and New Zealand Parties while successfully exposing the divisions within the National Party. It was able to argue that its work was only half completed, and promised that the controversial economic policies would pay dividends within the lifetime of the next government. But the government also relied heavily on the nuclear ships ban to bolster its support. Its most effective election broadcasts and advertisments were those which focused on the ships-ban and were complemented by widespread 'vote nuclear-free' campaigns by peace and disarmament groups in the country. One full-page newspaper advertisment declared just three days prior to the election: 'This country must stay nuclear free – don't go back with the bombs. Come forward with us. Be there with Labour.'[57] The New Zealand electorate clearly took heed of this message when they cast their votes, and in so doing provided a powerful vindication of the nuclear-free policies pursued by the Labour government during the previous three years.

56. Ibid., p. 72.
57. *The Press* (Christchurch), 12 August 1987.

Conclusions

There is a sense in which conclusions to this book are difficult to draw, for at the time of writing, the dispute between New Zealand and its ANZUS partners continues.[1] Nevertheless, the ships-ban survived a second general election and seems likely to be maintained for some years. Some lessons can certainly be learnt from this and explanations for its success offered.

But in heralding its 'success', there is a tendency perhaps to overlook the contradictions which the New Zealand nuclear-free policy has yet to confront. It may therefore be useful to look at those contradictions inherent in the nuclear-free policy *as it stands*, and to suggest tentatively that simply because the ban on nuclear ships has remained intact in New Zealand that this does not necessarily mean that the United States has 'failed' in its objectives.

The New Zealand Perspective: Why was the Ships-Ban a Success?

The nuclear ships ban should not be seen in isolation but in the context of a longer-term development of a Pacific rather than a European or North American consciousness in New Zealand. The New Zealand experience may well have implications for the western alliance as a whole, but the New Zealand perspective on the event is increasingly Pacific. Bearing this in mind, there are, however, several discernible factors which help to

1. For the latest developments before going to press see the Afterword (pp. 169–70) below.

explain the success of the nuclear-free policy in New Zealand.

Of considerable importance is the small population base (3.2 million) which has meant that the peace and labour movements have been able to have an influence and presence in almost every area of New Zealand society which is proportionately much stronger than in most other countries. Personal contact has been a relatively important feature of group relations. The job of public education, reaching the media, and lobbying politicians is perhaps easier – and arguably more effective – than in countries such as Britain with a larger population. To give just one example, a member of parliament in New Zealand with a 2,000 vote majority is considered to be in a 'safe' seat, so self-interest alone dictates that the mood of constituents must be listened to attentively.

The development of the peace movement itself stretches back over many years and was vigorous in the mid-1970s. By contrast, in Europe, most anti-nuclear campaigning developed very rapidly in 1979 and 1980 from a very small base. With the exception of the neutron bomb controversy in the Netherlands and West Germany, there had been almost no anti-nuclear campaigning in Europe in the period 1964–79, so the massive expansion of the early 1980s had little basis of long-term support and interest.

By contrast, in the mid-1970s, anti-nuclear activists in New Zealand were able skilfully to capture news headlines with sea-borne protests against visiting nuclear warships and submarines, and simultaneously set the agenda for the nuclear debate which the land-based nuclear-free zone movement was taking to every town, city and village in the country. This activism itself was aided by a wider tradition of social protest which had developed in New Zealand, first against the country's involvement in the Vietnam War and the presence of US military bases in New Zealand, and later in relation to campaigning on apartheid. The Vietnam experience should not be underestimated. Antagonism to US policy towards Vietnam was considerable in Western Europe and the US itself, but in Australia and New Zealand there was the complication that service-people were fighting in a war which was essentially the policy of another government. Thus, for New Zealand, the experience related both to the country's involvement in a war of doubtful merit *and* to its relationship to the United States.

A further cause of concern prior to the 1980s was the 'nuclearisation' of the Pacific, especially in the form of French nuclear weapons tests. Again, there had been a history of protest against such operations, and part of the

158

concern had been with the environmental impact of these tests. This is reminiscent of the early anti-nuclear protests of the late 1950s, leading to the 'first wave' of CND and other organisations in Europe, which had its origins in the growing concern over the effects of the massive nuclear test programmes of the superpowers in the 1950s.

These various factors combined to ensure that the movement was at its strongest in the early 1980s, but built on foundations stretching over many years. It was further encouraged by the worldwide popular movements against nuclear arms and the election pledge of the Labour Party to ban nuclear warships from New Zealand ports should it be elected as the next government.

The receptivity of the New Zealand public to the ships-ban can also be explained – at least in part – by the country's geographical isolation. There are few perceived threats to New Zealand, and concern about the Soviet military is low in a region which is largely ideologically united. Contrast this with Western Europe where the threat from the Soviet Union was widely considered to be quite marked in the early 1980s. There, the fear of the Soviet threat was partially overtaken by a greater fear – of the growing risks and likely effects of a nuclear conflict – and this underpinned the anti-nuclear protests for several years. In New Zealand the low level of perception of a threat to security did not help proponents of nuclear policies in arguing for New Zealand involvement in US defence strategy through warship visits.

More specifically on the peace movement in New Zealand, it would appear that its decentralised, diverse and grassroots nature proved to be a considerable strength. As peace activist Kevin Hackwell has said: 'Because of the lack of centralised national structures, the politicians cannot make compromise deals with a peace movement power elite. Instead they have to deal with a large number of groups, and this usually occurs at the community level where it is most effective.'[2]

One could argue that there are some disadvantages in a decentralised movement, in that nationally-known 'peace movement personalities' can provide a focus for media debate, but they can also be involved in internal power politics, providing a useful focus for media antagonism. On balance, the experience of a decentralised peace movement appears to represent a powerful advantage to the development of anti-nuclear campaigning.

2. Kevin Hackwell, 'A Peace Movement Victory', *Sanity*, no. 1, January 1988, pp. 13–14.

A Break with the West?

While the nuclear ships ban seems, at first sight, to have been a success, the New Zealand nuclear-free legislation is not without its contradictions. We have seen on several occasions how David Lange and other government spokespeople laid great emphasis on New Zealand's nuclear-free policies not being incompatible with membership of the ANZUS Treaty and with an overall foreign policy alignment with the West.

However, to opt out of only the nuclear dimension of a security alliance with the United States is not only questionable morally but also impossible practically. There is considerable contradiction in the New Zealand policy as it stands. Indeed, the policy makes little moral or practical sense so long as New Zealand remains a member of ANZUS, which – even if not by a strict definition – is clearly a 'nuclear alliance' in a political and strategic sense. The United States global military strategy makes little or no distinction between its nuclear and non-nuclear components. The recurrent problem that arises in relation to ANZUS is that it has come to represent not only a tripartite *treaty*, but also an *alliance* between the three signatories. As a treaty, ANZUS is a legalistic document, but as an alliance it has come to represent a whole host of military, political and economic relationships between the three members. So by remaining in ANZUS, New Zealand has opened itself to the charge that it wants to enjoy the 'benefits' of an alliance without sharing the full costs of membership. Indeed, given that the Labour government showed no inclination to withdraw from the ANZUS alliance, their steadfastness in maintaining the ships-ban could be seen as stubborness or poor alliance management as much as a principled stand against nuclear weapons. Critics on the right have used this contradiction as a reason for abandoning the ships-ban, or at least adopting a Japanese-style 'ask no questions' nuclear-free policy, and returning to full military integration with the United States and Australia. Critics on the left have argued that it is a reason for New Zealand withdrawing from the ANZUS Treaty and adopting a neutral, non-aligned, or civilian-based defence and foreign policy.

A central argument is that the Labour government has maintained that the nuclear ships ban is based, at least in part, on a moral rejection of nuclear weapons and nuclear strategies. This being so it is therefore an equivocation to adopt the nuclear-free moral high ground whilst simultaneously espousing a pro-American foreign policy alignment. Since that alignment has an explicit nuclear component, it is possible to adopt one or the other, but the two together are irreconcilable. It has, in fact, been argued that the political and geo-strategic effect of the ships-ban and nuclear-free policies has been reduced because any contribution they make to world peace, arms control or disarmament is *incidental* and not central to them.

There is, then, some merit to the argument that the nuclear ships ban and nuclear-free legislation has not signalled a break from the 'West', nor a challenge to the overall US military strategy in the Pacific and to assumptions of a Soviet threat to the region.

However, such a conclusion may be premature. Because of its past dependence on larger powers for protection – both in the marketplace and in defence – New Zealand has been constrained in its formulation of an independent foreign policy. Just as the country has been forced to find new markets for its exports since Britain's entry into the EEC, so too has it begun to question where its security interests lie. The two are inextricably linked. As M.N. Norrish, the Secretary of the New Zealand Department of Foreign Affairs, has reflected: 'You cannot adopt a position of chronic economic dependence on the one hand, and expect independent political relationships to blossom on the other.'[3]

But now that New Zealand has ceased to be an economic colony, there are also indications that the country is moving away from a 'psychological' dependence on powerful allies to defend it. In this context, the absence of any real military threat to New Zealand in the South West Pacific has led many to question the continuing purpose of ANZUS. Accordingly, it is seen by some as being more a reflection of New Zealand's hitherto political, cultural and economic subordination than of any military exigencies.

If New Zealand is moving away from this 'psychological' dependence on the West, then it may be assumed that ANZUS will have a decreasing significance in the formulation of its defence and foreign policy. This is certainly the view taken by several writers, including Norrish, who argues that the ships-ban and subsequent ANZUS dispute needs to be viewed in a longer time frame than many commentators have been prepared to acknowledge.[4] Thus, the principles which underlie the present direction of New Zealand's foreign policy can be squarely placed in the context of an evolutionary transformation from a colony to an independent nation.

3. M. Norrish, 'The Changing Context of New Zealand's Foreign Policy', *The Australian Quarterly*, vol. 58, no. 2, winter 1986, pp. 192–7.
4. Ibid.

When the decision to ban nuclear ships from New Zealand is seen in this historical context, it will be apparent that the policy was not some sort of aberration, but a logical and sequential step in the reappraisal of New Zealand's security interests. It has meant that New Zealand is – potentially at least – in a state of fundamental foreign policy change. It is nuclear-free, more independent than at any time in its post-colonial history, and forming trade and diplomatic ties with many more nations. The question remains, however, whether it will formally break the ANZUS umbilical cord. Most people in the peace movement, the Social Credit and New Zealand parties and large sections of the Labour Party would want this to happen, but the argument that New Zealand will be more effective in influencing US foreign policy if it remains in an alliance with the United States is one which continues to have much support.

Certainly, the New Zealand government has so far sought to continue close military links with its allies. While the United States curtailed many joint defence activities, such as naval exercises and training operations, New Zealand was able to maintain relations with other states within the western alliance, and Australia, in particular, seems to have been happy to fill many of the gaps left by the US actions.[5] Even Britain has continued, in a suitably low-key manner, to maintain good military relations, one example being the continuing New Zealand participation in the activities of the high-level Royal College of Defence Studies in London. US actions apart, there is as yet little sign of New Zealand turning away from military co-operation with its traditional allies.

The United States Perspective: Failure or Successful Damage Limitation?

Viewed from the perspective of the United States, what conclusions may be drawn from the ANZUS/ships-ban dispute with New Zealand? After the 1984 election, US policy towards New Zealand concerning the issue had three components: getting an immediate compromise on forthcoming warship visits; reversing the government's overall stand on nuclear affairs; and shifting public opinion away from its majority support for this stand. As we have seen, the United States did not seek to test the new policy

5. See, for example, Steve Hoadley, 'New Zealand's National Interests, Defence Capabilities and ANZUS', in Jacob Bercovitch (ed.), *ANZUS in Crisis: Alliance Management in International Affairs*, Macmillan, London, 1988.

immediately but allowed time for a compromise. When this failed, the *Buchanan* incident ushered in a period of quite intense political pressure and propaganda efforts, extending to threats of economic sanctions and, possibly, an involvement in some covert operations. Over a three-year period, the various efforts failed to have the desired effect and, in that respect, the US policy was a failure.

This was largely due to continuing public support, aided no doubt by the *Rainbow Warrior* incident, and by the counter-productive nature of many of the US actions. It may also be argued that the position of Australia was significant. While Prime Minister Bob Hawke himself was clearly opposed to the New Zealand government's stance, he was limited in his ability to exercise that opposition.[6] New Zealand's position on the nuclear issue had widespread support in Australia, especially among many elements of Hawke's own party. Moreover, there was a dislike of what appeared to be US bullying of a small country. A more dominantly right-wing government in Australia, strongly supportive of the United States, might have made Lange's domestic positon more difficult to sustain.

It is clear that the United States viewed the New Zealand government's nuclear-free policy with considerable antagonism. As we discussed earlier, this was in part due to the prevalent belief that the Pacific was dominantly an area of US influence, partly due to the exercising of the nuclear-free option against the US Navy, at the time the lynch-pin of the developing Maritime Strategy, and partly due to the fear that the New Zealand action would be contagious, both in the Pacific and also in Europe where public opposition to US nuclear strategy was already considerable. As a consequence, an unusually large effort was devoted to trying to ensure a change of policy in a country which might otherwise have been regarded as somewhat peripheral to US interests.

An initial conclusion is obviously that the US policy towards New Zealand failed, but changing the New Zealand stance may not have been the only aim. The very policies directed towards New Zealand were, in a sense,,directed towards many other allies, in that they demonstrated the concern with which the United States viewed an ally stepping out of line. Thus United States action against New Zealand was a warning to other countries.

It is far too early to say whether this has had a positive or negative

6. For a detailed analysis of Australian attitudes to denuclearisation, see Andrew Mack, 'Denuclearisation in Australia and New Zealand: Issues and Prospects', Working Paper No. 52, Peace Research Centre, Australian National University, Canberra, 1988.

effect, and the circumstances have changed greatly with the recent positive developments in Soviet arms control policy under Gorbachev and the completion of the Intermediate Nuclear Force (INF) agreement. Within Europe, that treaty has raised many issues concerning NATO nuclear doctrine, and has broadly encouraged European opinion in favour of further nuclear arms control. NATO has operated over the years on the basis of consensus, and that consensus has, on matters of nuclear policy, faithfully followed US policy.

In the late 1980s there have been signs of a change in attitude. There have been protracted negotiations over the status of US bases in Greece and, at the other end of the Mediterranean, Spain has negotiated the removal of a Tactical Fighter Wing of 72 nuclear-capable F–16 strike aircraft. The Spanish example is particularly interesting in that the Spanish government supported membership of NATO in a referendum with the proviso that the F–16s could be negotiated away. The referendum went in favour of NATO membership and negotiations with the US on the F–16 issue started shortly afterwards. The US appeared to enter the negotiations on the assumption that a compromise could be agreed which would allow the planes to stay, much as they had approached the Lange government in 1984 in the belief that a compromise on warship visits could be achieved. As in New Zealand, so in Spain, they were surprised by government persistence; a compromise could not be reached and the Spanish government required the United States to base the planes elsewhere.

In the spring of 1988, a general election was caused in Denmark over the issue of warship port visits and while the government of the day was narrowly returned to power and visits were allowed to continue, the election was close. A few months later, in October of that year, it proved very difficult for the NATO Nuclear Planning Group to persuade the uneasy coalition government of Belgium to accept a consensus communique which implied further nuclear modernisation in NATO. In West Germany, following the INF Treaty in 1987, a debate developed right across the political spectrum on the status of NATO tactical nuclear weapons.

It is very difficult to assess the extent to which the New Zealand experience had any impact on governments in Western Europe. The US pressures on New Zealand received some general media coverage and much more attention within the peace movements, and the 1987 election result was well received among anti-nuclear campaigners in Western

Europe. The governmental developments on the other hand were related at least in part to the changing attitudes in Europe following the INF Treaty, as well as to the pressures of domestic public opinion.

It is difficult, too, to assess the impact of the New Zealand experience on countries of the Pacific, but Australia and Japan are certainly far more significant to US strategy. It is debatable whether the United States totally miscalculated the strength of support in New Zealand for the nuclear-free policies, or whether their heavy-handed reprisals were undertaken in the certain knowledge and acceptance that they would fail in New Zealand, but be sufficient to dissuade other countries, especially in the Pacific, from following the New Zealand example. Perhaps New Zealand is considered an expendable ally if that is the price which has to be paid to prevent strategically more important countries such as Japan and Australia from adopting more than just token nuclear-free policies. Even so, in Australia the union opposition to the visit of the Royal Navy's nuclear-capable aircraft-carrier *Ark Royal* in October 1988 shows that opposition to nuclear-armed ships continues, albeit not by government.

The United States can claim that even if it did fail to reverse the ships-ban policy and prevent the nuclear-free legislation in New Zealand, a wider aim of punishing the Lange government, whilst keeping the framework of the ANZUS alliance together and 'warning' other allies, was successful. Where other countries have taken heart from the New Zealand stance, in the case of Fiji at least, nuclear-free aspirations have been short-lived.

What Lies Ahead?

With the re-election of the Lange government in August 1987, it is not clear what the longer-term reaction of the United States will be. The US Presidential election in the autumn of 1988 was a dull affair, with George Bush maintaining a substantial lead in the polls for the last few weeks of campaigning. Surprisingly, defence was not a central issue, although the perception of the United States as a 'nation reborn to greatness' was a strong feature of the Bush campaign.

While a somewhat populist style of patriotism was encouraged, it seems likely that the evolution of East–West relations in the near future will be determined more by Moscow than Washington. President Gorbachev's UN speech in December 1988, announcing major unilateral disarmament measures, was one part of a much longer-term Soviet policy.

If trends set in motion under Mr Gorbachev from 1985 to 1988 continue, it is going to become much more difficult for the 'Soviet threat' to be used to justify high levels of defence spending in the West and perhaps even aspects of nuclear policy. One reason for the New Zealand Labour government's success in maintaining the nuclear-free policy was that the Soviet Union was, at best, a distant threat to New Zealand. If the threat recedes from Europe, then the New Zealand nuclear-free contagion could well spread.

For New Zealand itself, it is likely that the United States will grudgingly accept that the nuclear-free legislation is there to stay, and will concentrate instead on remaining 'friends' if not 'allies'. Certainly, it is difficult to see what further overt reprisals the United States can take against New Zealand except perhaps punitive trade sanctions – which would do little to engender public support for the United States in New Zealand. The British, if the experience of the first three years is anything to go by, will wait and see what the Americans do, and then echo it. They, at least, will not rock the boat.

The New Zealand government itself has an opportunity to extend its anti-nuclear outlook into new dimensions and could, by doing so, meet criticisms of its lack of a full commitment to a nuclear-free world. At the global level there is an extensive agenda. The negotiation of a Comprehensive Test Ban Treaty is an immediate priority, especially in view of the extensive current research into third-generation nuclear warheads. Progress in strategic nuclear arms reduction, through START 1 and START 2 treaties, should include the control of deployment of new weapons, especially strategic counterforce weapons, and negotiations on intermediate and tactical nuclear weapons must include the important area of naval nuclear arms control. The Non Proliferation Treaty is due for review in 1990, and requires considerable strengthening, and an anti-satellite weapons treaty and improved anti-ballistic missile treaty are other requirements. Nuclear-free zones have particular applications in the Pacific and Indian Oceans, and the developments in conventional force projection noted earlier in this book have also to be brought under some kind of control.

It is apparent that New Zealand could have a general role in the encouragement of some of these processes and a highly specific role in certain cases. Thus, its voice should be raised in any appropriate international forum on questions such as test bans and a nuclear weapons freeze, as well as space weapons and the control of proliferation. It has a particular geographical interest in relation to warhead and missile testing as well as ballistic missile submarine deployments in Pacific waters. It has a highly specific interest in matters such as the control of incidents at sea and the development of the nuclear-free zone concept in its region.

It would be appropriate for New Zealand to work with other countries in order to create broadly-based pressures on the existing major nuclear powers, and such international co-operation should not be solely regional. New Zealand's existing cultural and political links with North America, Europe and the Commonwealth should be utilised as just one part of the much larger process of fostering a global climate favouring nuclear arms control, disarmament and military disengagement.

Such a process requires diplomatic persuasion and negotiation from a basis of considerable knowledge and expertise. It requires the development of appropriate units in foreign affairs and defence departments, backed up by a substantial increase in applied research in universities. Such developments should be vigorously promoted by government and this could well extend to an endowed national peace research institute, possibly along the lines of the Stockholm International Peace Research Institute with an international board of governors, but regional co-operation with other Pacific states creating a system of linked research units in several countries might be more appropriate.

An active policy of diplomacy, supported by the necessary research, could underpin a substantial contribution by New Zealand, building on its existing commitment to a nuclear-free future. It is not unknown for countries to exert an influence out of proportion to their economic and political power. New Zealand would be an appropriate and positive addition.

The criticism made earlier of the limitations of New Zealand's nuclear-free policies should not detract from the importance of the nuclear ships ban and the subsequent nuclear-free legislation. Implementation of these policies required considerable political courage and resilience in the face of bitter criticism and pressure from some of New Zealand's so-called allies.

Such was the level of popular support for the ships-ban after the 1987 election that it is questionable whether a future New Zealand government would be willing to revoke it. And with the ban codified in law, any future attempt to overturn it will have to be done in the full glare of parliamentary and public scrutiny. It is perhaps more likely that the ban will form the basis for New Zealand foreign and defence policy for a long time yet.

Without wishing to detract from the 'narrow' objective of keeping nuclear weapons out of New Zealand, perhaps the true significance of the Labour government's action will only be appreciated with the benefit of historical hindsight. Over sixty years ago, the *New Zealand Herald* wrote: 'All is yet molten, mercurial. There are more departures to make than precedents to follow. To have a history is an old land's glory and safeguard: to make history is a new land's perilous employment.'[7]

In the longer time frame that is needed, it remains to be seen whether the ships-ban and subsequent nuclear-free legislation have represented a departure in New Zealand's history, or whether in a few years time nuclear warheads will again be welcome in New Zealand's territorial waters. But as we have discussed earlier, the opportunity now exists for New Zealand to consolidate its nuclear-free status and use this to develop a peacemaking role in the Pacific and further afield.

7. Quoted in Keith Sinclair, *A History of New Zealand*, Penguin Books, London, 1959, p. 301.

Afterword

At the time of writing this afterword (May 1989), the dispute between New Zealand and the United States continues, albeit in a more low-key fashion since the 1987 general election. Something of an uneasy stalemate now exists, and in New Zealand the debate has moved beyond the immediate ramifications of the nuclear ships ban to a longer-term assessment of the future needs of New Zealand's armed forces, and in particular the navy.

The Lange government has been considering replacing the present *Leander* frigates in the New Zealand Navy with up to four new frigates built by Australia at a cost of over NZ$2 billion. In the light of the 1987 Defence Review, which emphasised a more modest role for the New Zealand armed forces, the proposed purchase of these state-of-the-art frigates has caused much controversy. The cost of the frigates alone gives an indication of their (over) sophistication, and only if New Zealand were to become involved in high intensity naval warfare would their advanced weapon systems make sense. No such scenario is envisaged by either the New Zealand government nor by the Ministry of Defence. A strong and widely supported campaign against the purchase of the frigates has been waged in New Zealand, and it is far from certain that the government will decide to purchase them. It is possible that cheaper and less sophisticated vessels, which are more suited to the post-ANZUS role of the New Zealand Navy, will be brought from a European ship-builder instead.

We suggested in the 'Conclusions' that the United States would grudgingly accept that the nuclear-free policies of the Labour government would remain. This has been epitomised by the replacement of Paul

169

Cleveland as US Ambassador in Wellington. Cleveland, who, it will be recalled, was a career diplomat, adopted a high profile in the ships-ban dispute. However, his replacement Della Newman is a political appointee to the post, her main qualification for the job being that she chaired George Bush's presidential campaign in Washington. Even so, her ignorance of New Zealand politics and US–New Zealand relations is surprising. Interviewed in February soon after her appointment was announced, she was unable to name New Zealand's present prime minister, and confessed to knowing very little about the country. Furthermore, she said that she had no particular interest in foreign affairs.[1]

During a visit to the United States in April 1989, David Lange spoke at Yale University, and caused a storm of controversy when he suggested that New Zealand might formally withdraw from the ANZUS Council of Ministers. On the relationship between New Zealand and the United States, he said: 'There is not and cannot be any security alliance between the United States and New Zealand. There can be no going back to the way it was. . . . This raises the issue of whether New Zealand should give formal notice of withdrawal from the ANZUS Council.'[2] The speech surprised both his cabinet colleagues and the United States who claimed to have had no forewarning of its content, and it served to sharpen criticism of Lange's style of leadership.

In fact, most other major developments since the 1987 general election have centred on the internal problems which have beset the Labour government, and particularly on the leadership of David Lange. Faced with growing criticism of the government's monetarist economic policies, Lange sacked the architect of the economic reforms, Roger Douglas, in December 1988. The Minister for State-Owned Enterprises, Richard Prebble, met a similar fate after attacking Lange for his 'presidential style' of leadership, including his propensity for announcing policy decisions without consulting the cabinet. By sacking two of his ministers who were politically to the right of the party, Lange believed that he could win back the support of those many party members and voters who were disillusioned with the rightward shift in Labour's policies since 1984. However, the belief that the Labour Party had abandoned its traditional principles in almost every sphere of government (save the nuclear ships ban) led the Labour MP and former President of the Party, Jim Anderton, to form a

1. Cited in 'Would-be Envoy Vague on PM', *The Press*, 9 February 1989.
2. David Lange, 'The Nuclear Issue and Relations Between Great Powers and Small States', George Herbert Jnr Lecture, Yale University, 25 April 1989.

new political party of the left in May 1989 called the New Labour Party. The early indications suggest that the party may attract considerable support.

In contrast, an opinion poll taken just after Anderton had left the Labour Party revealed that of those respondents committed to a political party, only 30 per cent would vote Labour, compared with 63 per cent for the opposition National Party.[3] Even taking into account the large percentage of undecided voters (over 30 per cent), it will take a considerable turnaround before the 1990 general election for the Labour government to reverse what some commentators are describing as a potentially terminal decline in support. And it must be doubtful if the public support for the nuclear ships ban could be galvanised again at the eleventh hour to re-elect the Labour government, though it may well be sufficiently strong to prevent a future National Party government reversing the country's nuclear-free stance.

Postscript: As this book was going to press, David Lange unexpectedly resigned as New Zealand Prime Minister on 7 August 1989. His successor, Geoffrey Palmer, may initiate changes in the Labour government's social and economic policies but is unlikely to alter the overall foreign policy of the government, and in particular the nuclear ships ban.

3. Cited in 'Labour hits low in Poll', *New Zealand News UK*, 17 May 1989, p. 10.

The ANZUS Treaty

Security Treaty
Between
Australia, New Zealand, and the United States of America

The Parties to this Treaty,

Reaffirming their faith in the purposes and principles of the Charter of the United Nations and their desire to live in peace with all peoples and all Governments, and desiring to strengthen the fabric of peace in the Pacific Area,

Noting that the United States already has arrangements pursuant to which its armed forces are stationed in the Philippines, and has armed forces and administrative responsibilities in the Ryukyus, and upon the coming into force of the Japanese Peace Treaty may also station armed forces in and about Japan to assist in the preservation of peace and security in the Japan Area,

Recognizing that Australia and New Zealand as members of the British Commonwealth of Nations have military obligations outside as well as within the Pacific Area,

Desiring to declare publicly and formally their sense of unity, so that no potential aggressor could be under the illusion that any of them stand alone in the Pacific Area, and

Desiring further to coordinate their efforts for collective defense for the preservation of peace and security pending the development of a more comprehensive system of regional security in the Pacific Area,

Therefore declare and agree as follows:

Article I

The Parties undertake, as set forth in the Charter of the United Nations, to settle any international disputes in which they may be involved by peaceful means in such a manner that international peace and security and justice are not endangered and to refrain in their international relations from the threat or use of force in any manner inconsistent with the purposes of the United Nations.

Article II

In order more effectively to achieve the objective of this Treaty the Parties separately and jointly by means of continuous and effective self-help and mutual aid will maintain and develop their individual and collective capacity to resist armed attack.

Article III

The Parties will consult together whenever in the opinion of any of them the territorial integrity, political independence or security of any of the Parties is threatened in the Pacific.

Article IV

Each Party recognizes that an armed attack in the Pacific Area on any of the Parties would be dangerous to its own peace and safety and declares that it would act to meet the common danger in accordance with its constitutional processes.

Any such armed attack and all measures taken as a result thereof shall be immediately reported to the Security Council of the United Nations. Such measures shall be terminated when the Security Council has taken the measures necessary to restore and maintain international peace and security.

Article V

For the purpose of Article IV, an armed attack on any of the Parties is deemed to include an armed attack on the metropolitan territory of any of the Parties, or on the island territories under its jurisdiction in the Pacific or on its armed forces, public vessels or aircraft in the Pacific.

Article VI

This Treaty does not affect and shall not be interpreted as affecting in any way the rights and obligations of the Parties under the Charter of the United Nations or the responsibility of the United Nations for the maintenance of international peace and security.

Article VII

The Parties hereby establish a Council, consisting of their Foreign Ministers or their Deputies, to consider matters concerning the implementation of this Treaty. The Council should be so organized as to be able to meet at any time.

Article VIII

Pending the development of a more comprehensive system of regional security in the Pacific Area and the development by the United Nations of more effective means to maintain international peace and security, the Council, established by Article VII, is authorized to maintain a consultative relationship with States, Regional Organisations, Associations of States or other authorities in the Pacific Area in a position to further the purposes of this Treaty and to contribute to the security of that Area.

Article IX

This Treaty shall be ratified by the Parties in accordance with their respective constitutional processes. The instruments of ratification shall be deposited as soon as possible with the Government of Australia, which will notify each of the other signatories of such deposit. The Treaty shall enter into force as soon as the ratifications of the signatories have been deposited.

Article X

This Treaty shall remain in force indefinitely. Any Party may cease to be a member of the Council established by Article VII one year after notice has been given to the Government of Australia, which will inform the Governments of the other Parties of the deposit of such notice.

Article XI

This Treaty in the English language shall be deposited in the archives of the Government of Australia. Duly certified copies thereof will be transmitted by that Government to the Governments of each of the other signatories.

IN WITNESS WHEREOF the undersigned Plenipotentiaries have signed this Treaty.
DONE at the city of San Francisco this first day of September, 1951.

FOR AUSTRALIA:
     PERCY C. SPENDER
FOR NEW ZEALAND:
     C.A. BERENDSEN
FOR THE UNITED STATES OF AMERICA:
     DEAN ACHESON
     JOHN FOSTER DULLES
     ALEXANDER WILEY
     JOHN J. SPARKMAN

Select Bibliography

Alves, D., *Anti-nuclear Attitudes in New Zealand and Australia*, US Government Printing Office, Washington, 1985

Ambrose, Stephen E., *Rise to Globalism: American Foreign Policy 1938–80*, Penguin Books, London and New York, 1980

Bercovitch, Jacob (ed.), *ANZUS in Crisis: Alliance Management in International Affairs*, Macmillan, London, 1988

Clements, Kevin, 'New Zealand's Relations with the UK, the US and the Pacific', *Alternatives* (New York), vol. 14, winter 1986, pp. 595f.

'Defence and Security: What New Zealanders Want', report of the Defence Committee of Enquiry, July 1986, Government Printer, Wellington, 1986

Gold, Hyam (ed.), *New Directions In New Zealand Foreign Policy*, Benton Ross Auckland, 1985

Harford, Barbara (ed.), *Beyond ANZUS – Alternatives for Australia, New Zealand and the Pacific*, Beyond ANZUS Committee, Peace Movement Aotearoa, Wellington, 1985

Henderson, John, et al., *Beyond New Zealand: The Foreign Policy of a Small State*, Reed Methuen, Auckland, 1980

Holsti, K.J., *International Politics*, 3rd edn, Prentice-Hall, London, 1983

Hubbard, Anthony, 'The Sinking of the Buchanan', *The Dominion Sunday Times*, 29 March 1987

Mack, Andrew, 'Denuclearisation in Australia and New Zealand: Issues and Prospects', Working Paper No. 52, Australian National University Peace Research Centre, Canberra, 1988

McLaughlin, Murray, 'The Campaign to set New Zealand Thinking the USA Way', *New Zealand Sunday Times*, 30 November 1986, p. 5

McMillan, Stuart, *Neither Confirm Nor Deny – The nuclear ships dispute between New Zealand and the United States*, Allen & Unwin/Port Nicholson Press, Wellington, 1987

177

Newnham, Tom, *Peace Squadron – The Sharp End of Nuclear Protest in New Zealand*, Graphic Publications, Auckland, 1986

Norrish, M., 'The Changing Context of New Zealand's Foreign Policy', *The Australian Quarterly*, vol. 58, no. 2, winter 1986, pp. 192–7

Robson, Alan, 'New Zealand's Anti-Nuclear Cold War', School of Social and Economic Development, Working Paper No. 3, University of the South Pacific, Suva, Fiji, 1986

Thomson, Warren, et al., *Old Myths or New Options: The New Zealand Security Debate After the Nuclear Ships Ban*, Defence Alternatives Study Group, Christchurch [1988]

Wilkes, Owen, 'Stooging Around the Cook Islands – The Mysterious Case of the Disappearing Submarine', *New Zealand Monthly Review*, vol. XXVII, no. 292, October 1986

——, 'Down Under With the CIA', *ENDpapers Sixteen* (incorporating the *END Bulletin of the Bertrand Russell Peace Foundation* and the *Spokesman*), *Spokesman* 54, Summer 1987

Index